SOCIOLOGY AS A SPIRITUAL PRACTICE

How Studying People Can Make You a Better Person

Christopher Pieper, Ph.D.

Cover image © Shutterstock, Inc.

Kendall Hunt
publishing company

www.kendallhunt.com
Send all inquiries to:
4050 Westmark Drive
Dubuque, IA 52004-1840

Copyright © 2015 by Christopher Pieper

ISBN 978-1-4652-7012-2

Printed in the United States of America

CONTENTS

Prologue

The Vision

"Sociology is not a practice, but an attempt to understand."

—*Peter Berger,* An Invitation to Sociology

Claire was not happy. In one of the slightly comfortable chairs facing my desk, she was putting me on notice: My course, Introduction to Sociology, she explained, was wrecking her plan. "All I ever wanted was a basic suburban life," she went on. "Two or three kids, lawn sprinklers, husband with a good job, dinner at Applebee's now and then...you know, nothing weird." Now, she said, all of that sounds unappealing, even wrong.

"What do you mean, Claire?" I inquired. "It was not my intent to upset you. My goal is just to show you what we do in our field."

"Right, but now a lot of things I used to know were true are uncertain, and a lot of my beliefs I can't believe anymore. I always knew the world was messed up, but now I realize I'm part of the problem. I just can't go about my life pretending it will all go away," she continued.

"So, what do you plan to do?" I pressed.

Claire paused pensively. "Not sure," she mumbled. "I just want to help people."

The inspiration for this book came through experiences just like this one. After several years of teaching large introductory courses, I noticed an increasing number of students coming to office hours recounting stories of how "sociology is making me a more caring person" "your class is showing me how everyone and everything is connected" or "this course has helped me grow in my spiritual life." I was frankly surprised by this reaction. Though I study religion sociologically and occasionally include spiritual or religious cases in lectures, it was not my intent to convey these themes in the course. So, in typical social science fashion, I began to carefully track how many students seemed to be affected in this way and the specific effects themselves. Over time, I observed a clear trajectory in the following direction:

- Increased global awareness and moral responsibility
- Greater personal responsibility for social issues
- Increased empathy, particularly those very different from them
- Decrease in prejudice and fear of unfamiliar groups
- Greater appreciation for complex causes
- A view of the self which is flexible and adaptive
- Decreased ego-centrism

I recognized these side-effects as basically identical with the necessary ingredients for healthy, humane societies—which was encouraging in itself—but also in line with the core ethical teachings of most of the world's great spiritual traditions. In a phrase: both social science and the great spiritual traditions are techniques of revealing the true nature of the self and the world around us.

Thus, a seed was planted.

That germ was nurtured through the other half of my vocation, that of social science research. A renewed interest in microsociology revealed the parallels between the view of self as essentially a social product and the view of most Eastern traditions that the Self is fundamentally impermanent and constantly in flux. Macrosociology also reveals this pattern. Structuration theory, for example, stresses how individual action creates the social order which then reshapes the individual. This view bears a strong family resemblance to the Christian doctrine of the "mystical body of Christ" and the Buddhist teaching on "codependent origination." Even what sociologists choose to study reflects the similarity. For example, the largest research area for several decades has been forms of inequality—economic, gender, racial, political, etc.—but why? A vastly over-simplified (but accurate) answer would be: because it hurts people. This is the same motive at the heart of every spiritual tradition, teaching the moral necessity of fairness.

I was struck however, by how the moral and spiritual dimensions of these endeavors had been mostly obscured under the veneer of so-called objective scientific dispassion. It appeared social scientists were ashamed of the emotional and humane motivations for their work. Are we to believe that Marxists spilled rivers of ink about the ravages of capitalism on workers merely because it was fascinating? Could it be that health demographers dedicate years of concentrated effort isolating the social causes and effects of illness simply to get to the bottom of the problem, as one would work on a crossword puzzle or math problem? The more sociologists I met, and the more of the discipline I practiced myself, the more it became clear that the motivations and objectives of social science coincided in unexpected ways with those of the spiritual paths. I therefore find myself in disagreement with my colleague Peter Berger, whose words begin this chapter. Sociology is both an attempt to understand and a practice. That practice, I argue, has spiritual fruits.

The road between social science and spirituality is two-way. In what follows, we shall investigate how enjoyable and productive journeys between them might be taken up. Consider this a map for the trip.

And along the way, we might even learn how to better "help some people," as Claire said. Or even if we're fortunate, to become better people.

CHAPTER ONE

The Spirit of Sociology

"Science is not only compatible with spirituality;
it is a profound source of spirituality."

—*Carl Sagan*

We live in an age when science and spirituality are seen as nearly opposite paths. Countless texts explore the tension between what has been called "sense and soul," "head and heart," or "rationality versus sentimentality."[1] Exponents from each camp have also joined in the discourse, with the "soul" side arguing that science is a threat to spirituality, disenchanting the world and explaining away transcendent experience rather than merely explaining it. The "sense" side contends that spiritual traditions are the real danger, miring social progress in superstition and emotionalism.

The tension goes beyond the public sphere too. Intellectuals have long contended that the fundamental assumptions and methods of science and spirituality are incompatible. Science operates from empiricism—that which can be observed and measured is real. Conversely, spirituality operates from experientialism—many things are real that can only be subjectively felt. The difference is in where one puts the emphasis: externally, where data can be verified by observers, or internally, where the description offered by those affected is deemed sufficient.

Given these basic differences, it's not surprising that many have given up hope of a reconciliation between science and spirituality. Some have taken the position articulated by paleontologist Stephen Jay Gould, that of "non-over-lapping magisteria," wherein science and spirituality are both seen as valuable and rich ways of knowing, but should have no traffic between them.[2] When the tension is interpreted less combatively, this is the common resting place for most on the subject, a kind of "live and let live" approach.

In this book I make the case that overlap between science and spirituality is not only desirable, but already present. First, the practice of social science is in many ways a spiritual discipline, and likewise that spiritual practice instills a sociological imagination. Secondly, the spiritual practice of sociology bears fruit in real, measurable ways through increased empathy, a greater appreciation for living, and a desire to serve others. The former is an argument of inherent compatibility, the latter a presentation of practical benefits.

Terms in this arena are often bandied about carelessly. To be sure, what counts as spiritual has as many meanings as practitioners. For current purposes, I define **spirituality** *as a state of being that transcends material forms, rationality, and the ego.* Spirituality would be meaningless if not for spiritual experiences, which are also notoriously hard to pin down. I define **spiritual experience** *as a profound interior experience of connection, bliss, insight, and a desire to trans-form oneself to maintain these interior states.* Thus, most spiritual experiences become spiritual practices. By **spiritual practice**, I mean a *regular, intentional activity designed to cultivate ultimate meaning, moral development, and enduring well-being.* This articulation speaks to the many interpretations of the term from religious, mystical, psychological, and secular perspectives.

Spiritual experiences, it should be stressed, are not the unique domain of religion or spiritual virtuosos. Natural scientists as celebrated and influential as Niels Bohr (quantum physics), Albert Einstein (relativity), Francis Crick (genetics), and Sam Harris (neuroscience) have all written beautifully about their own encounters with a sensation they identify as spiritual in the pursuit of knowledge in their own fields.[3,4,5] Frequently they describe an overwhelming feeling of awe, wonder, excitement, beauty, and gratitude. In every case, these experiences were abrupt, intrusive, and a total surprise. William James pro-duced the finest catalog of these experiences nearly a century ago, and it appears the core subjective phenomenon is the same, regardless of context or trigger.[6]

Spiritual experiences and the spiritual practices they inspire are a birthright of human personhood.

As this book is intended mainly for those just beginning their exploration of the field, it is designed, ironically, to also *humanize* the study of human behavior. How is it dehumanized? Too often, the tone, topics, and methods of many introductory textbooks, and even well-meaning lectures, erase or subordinate the "soul" of social science. This is frequently the result of two opposite processes with the same ultimate effect.

The first is to effectively transform human beings and social groups into variables. You and I are no longer individuals with names but aggregations of demographic traits such as age, gender, race, income, education level, and so on. Or we are merely the members (or worse "imprints") of the groups we happen to belong to, such as our political parties, religious affiliations, geographic region, or ethnic background. This reductionist variablizing often leaves students thinking of social dynamics as anything but dynamic. Sociology is depicted as a branch of mathematics, with a vague determinism underlying. In its harshest form, it has the effect of abstracting away all semblance of agency, freedom, creativity, and, well, humanity. Students rightly bristle at this suggestion, and may even reject social science altogether because of it.

The second technique is achieved not through reductionism but through an exaggerated structuralism. Here, social life is described as dominated by massive impersonal forces. "Society," a term which has a residue of vitality and community left in it, is replaced with "social structure," which connotes something faceless, overwhelming, and fixed. This structure is not only barely human, but is also astonishingly powerful, even controlling. Social structure was here before us and will be here after we are gone. Furthermore, this structure works through "social forces" that are as mysterious as they are potent. What kind of structures and forces do I mean? Globalization, heteronormativity, recidivism, the cycle of poverty, Fordism, secularization, de-skilling, and cultural imperialism are just a tiny fraction of candidates to name. Though not wrong, this overstructural approach is partial at best, and if not balanced by a look at the many instances of structural change and the human agents behind it, will leave students with an inaccurate and ugly image of the world and the future. On many occasions, I have personally heard students complain that sociology is "the antidote to hope" as a result this overstructural perspective. Probably more than a few professional sociologists have fallen prey to this view, as well.

These two divergent approaches converge to produce a common result: a social science is that is highly unsociable, a picture of ourselves that most of us do not recognize and would not want to study. Here I wish to advance an image of sociology (and social science generally) that preserves the holistic integrity of real human beings: sensitive, imaginative, fleshed out individuals who are both more than their traits and victims of the system. I hold that sociology at its best already has the capacity to do this, but it is at present a minority position. I aim to foreground these latent aspects and argue for the emphatic assertion of them throughout the discipline, both in research and teaching.

At the same time, I hope to reveal the sociological dimensions of spiritual traditions. After more than a decade of dedicated observation and practice, I am convinced that *every spiritual path contains and enacts a social theory*. Spiritual traditions are organized around and act out of a set of postulates about human beings and their collective activity. Few recognize their underlying social theories, though they often form the foundation of all further beliefs and prescriptions for behavior. Even fewer are cognizant of the sociological factors involved in their creation (historical context and economic position being just a couple), nor are they mindful of the social implications of these ideas upon contact with the outer cultural milieu. I do not claim special knowledge or forecasting on this front either. However, as a sociologist I can at least suggest a few helpful new lenses through which to view these folk social theories and their probable effects on real human beings and their communities.

Similarly, spiritual paths are often characterized as rooted in irrationality. This attack is often leveled by those focusing on the vast array of beliefs that spiritual and religious practitioners adhere to. A short list would include the commonly held beliefs in an afterlife (heaven, hell, purgatory, *bardo* realms, rebirth, reincarnation), revered ancestors and holy persons with whom believers communicate (saints, prophets, patriarchs, *bodhisattvas*, lamas, gurus), and miracles and other supernatural acts (virgin birth, splitting seas, resurrection, creating objects out of thin air). These claims are generally beyond the scope of empirical science to validate, though valiant and fascinating attempts have been made.[7,8] On the basis of their inability to "prove" what they believe in, spiritual traditions are frequently rejected, baby with bathwater, in postmodern, scientistic cultures. Look no further than Europe, once the very cradle of Christendom.

This criticism of spirituality needs to be put it in its proper place. For on the whole, the everyday lives of most followers are not directly steered by such supraempirical ideas, but by the ordinary benefits conveyed by spiritual and religious life. These include ethical and moral guidance, a community of loving and supportive people, a feeling of belonging through shared history and ritual, and most importantly, a "sacred canopy," which provides meaning and order in a chaotic and sometimes hostile world.[9] This, at least to me, is profoundly rational.

In my view, spiritual traditions survive and continue to be sought out because they satisfy in a unique way this human thirst for meaning and deeper value. They harmonize the tiny individual with the enormous cosmos and audaciously answer: "You matter." Science, philosophy, capitalism, art, and psychology have their own ways of attempting this harmonization, but seemingly always with less satisfying effects. It appears the individual desires to be significant, but also to know itself as part of a larger meaningful whole. Likewise, the Self wishes to be loved but also to give itself to something, someone else to love. This is the mystery of humanity, and spirituality has been the path to which most human beings have turned to find the ultimately rewarding answers. That billions have done so suggests it is either rational action or that as a species we are driven by more than reason and survival. My vote is for both.

Chapter Two

Self

"The problem with introspection is that it has no end."
—Philip K. Dick

Not many topics in sociology enjoy broad consensus. Scholars frequently disagree on core ideas in the discipline, such as whether culture or social structure is more decisive in the creation of inequality, the role of biological versus social factors on gender differences, whether religion will survive post-modernity, and if race is empirically "real" or socially constructed. At annual conferences, one even encounters debates on whether these issues should be core ideas or not. Diversity of perspective is commonplace in all academic fields, and is generally a positive force, when not taken to extremes.

An exception to this pattern is on the topic of the self. Since the genesis of microsociology and symbolic interactionism in the early 20th century, sociologists have on the whole accepted without serious opposition the fundamental presuppositions of those scholars regarding the self. A brief summary of those conclusions:

1. The "self" is fluid and without "essence"
2. The "self" is largely a product of social interaction (thus, no society, no self)
3. The self constricts and expands depending on social conditions, (thus capable of producing both wild narcissism and total fatalism)

4. The "self" is highly adaptive and "performed" within a context of constant feedback.

5. The self is actually many "selves," some of which may in high tension with other selves, leading to both internal and external problems (as well as delights).

Scholars working on the border between sociology and psychology were among the first to explore the self as a socio-scientific concept. Charles Horton Cooley introduced the useful notion of the "looking glass self" to refer to the process by which self-images were constructed from information provided by others as they interacted with the self.[10] Self-image, then, was impossible without social interaction. Prior to this innovation, the prevailing idea was that the self was a preexistent personal object, merely the exterior version of "I." Cooley provided rich empirical descriptions and a compelling causal narrative to show how the self was far from a static psychological entity. Instead, the self was more like a fluid composite of actions, first by the individual, followed by feedback from others, and then reflexive follow-up actions by the actor. The self was thus highly dynamic, a work in progress, and most importantly, constantly shaped and reshaped by social forces. In addition to having empirical grounding, Cooley's theory also enjoyed intuitive appeal. Any actual living human (especially adolescents) are painfully aware of the shifting and experimental nature of their "self," even moment to moment in some cases. These personal intuitions now had scientific credibility due to the insights of Cooley and his followers.

Cooley's work on the constructed nature of the self dovetailed well with the more elaborate explorations into the self provided by the first and most influential social psychologist, George Herbert Mead. Mead's groundbreaking work in *Mind, Self, and Society* remains classic reading in sociology and psychology today, in no small measure to his ingenious recognition that these three seemingly very different levels of analysis—the mental, the individual, and the collective—interpenetrate and shape each other.[11] Central to Mead's framework is the distinction between the "I" and the "me." The latter is that special version of the self that is almost entirely a product of social interaction. But he stressed too that the "me" is also produced for society; that is, it is called out of the individual by social contexts. This second point implies, akin to Cooley, that in the absence of society, a portion of the human person that we moderns regard as essential would never take shape. Natural experiments with feral humans have repeatedly shown this to be the case. Society, to put it rather baldly, creates the self.

The ramifications of this seemingly innocent insight could hardly be larger. The entire field of psychotherapy (and a good chunk of psychology itself) is concerned with problems of the self. What if this self, which psychology had held as synonymous with the mind and the individual, is actually a social phenomenon? Does this not suggest that self-problems are at least in part social problems? Aren't therefore social conditions partially to blame for whatever ailments human claim are emanating from their "selves"? A growing proportion of therapists, sociologists of health, psychologists, and social workers have found this to be the case in the last 20 years, but the seeds of their discoveries were planted nearly a century ago by Mead.

In the 1950s and 1960s, a new generation of sociologists had extended the pioneering work of Mead and Cooley with even richer empirical territory. It may come as a surprise to contemporary sociologists (and even a few normal people) that one of the best-selling nonfiction books of that period was the ungainly titled *The Presentation of Self in Everyday Life* by sociologist Erving Goffman.[12] Goffman's idea was a social science elaboration of Jaques' monologue from Shakespeare's *As You Like It*:

> *All the world's a stage,*
> *And all the men and women merely players.*
> *They have their exits and their entrances,*
> *And one man in his time plays many parts*[13]

For Goffman, social life was performance. His approach, wonderfully dubbed "dramaturgical analysis" after the stage hand responsible for the minutia of convincing performances, was also built on the premise that the self is a deeply influenced by contexts. Goffman took his constructionist argument farther than his predecessors, however, not only was the self a product of and for society, it was also a deliberate creation. Here, the social actor (a term used since the earliest days of sociology) is literally acting, in the stagecraft sense. Goffman dissected for the first time every detail of social interaction, in the process inaugurating the field of microsociology. For example, a woman preparing to go to work in the morning is not choosing an outfit, but a wardrobe or costume. Her Prada purse, cosmetic eyeglasses, crucifix key ring, and Beatles iPhone case? All strategic "props" to make her performance more convincing. That exaggerated formal speaking style and deeper timbre in her voice is only used with her boss and customers. With her intimate female friends, she shifts into "like," "totally," and "whatever." Goffman's ingenious contribution to the sociology of the self allows us to see the manifold ways in which that fluid self-described by Mead is a kind of co-performance, delivered by the actor but carefully crafted moment to moment based on feedback from audiences. But here's the beauty part as they say in Jersey: those audiences are *also* actors, receiving constant input from their social environments and adjusting accordingly. Thus, all public encounters are co-performances, and therefore, public life is stagecraft.

Microsociology confronts us with the possibility that the self is a bit less real than we conventionally believe. This socially shaped, performed, and highly adaptive self is real to be sure, but not timeless, fixed, or innate. Its realness is instead grounded in its utility to navigate a wide and unpredictable variety of social contexts. The self that most of us cling to as identical to "I" is best conceived as a kind of patchwork of past approved performances, current probationary personae, a good bit of improvisation, and a highly attuned sense of social judgment.

One of the sociological subfields in which this idea is most clearly visible is gender. Since the 1980s, sociologists of gender have made the persuasive case that, contrary to traditional thinking, gender is best conceived as another type of performance. A key component of the self, (which is already deeply shaped by social interactions, feedback, and cultural expectations), one's gender is likewise an ongoing, dynamic sub-persona according to this view.[14,15] Recent research in sociobiology has clarified and indeed restricted the degree to which gender is pure construction and performance.[16] Nevertheless a clear consensus has emerged that the way one expresses "selves" along the spectrum between "masculinity" and "femininity" shifts with local context, life course changes, culture-wide transformations, among other factors.

This is not to suggest that these aspects of identity are trivial or inconsequential. Far from it, in fact. For most human beings, the construct called "self" is among the most sacred, protected, and important thing in their lives, if forced to be honest. Within this concept are things that many humans have and continue to sacrifice and die for, including religious beliefs, tribal allegiances of myriad variety (including sports team loyalties—have you ever seen a World Cup match?), aesthetic preferences (K-pop or doom metal?), romantic interests (BoHo handlebar mustache boy or Luke Bryan dualie truck cowboy?), food tastes (Meat Lovers or Veggie with white sauce on gluten-free crust?), and most other facets of our individuality that make life interesting and passionate.

I am the Self.
Right?

At least in the modern West, on this question there is no doubt. As the Quebecois novelist Andre Berthiaume famously wrote, "We all wear masks, and the time comes when we cannot remove them without removing some of our own skin."[17]

It is a curious paradox that modern Westerners (and a growing number of non-Westerners) affirm two opposed ideas. On the one hand, the social and natural sciences are more than ever allied on the evidence that the Self is a convenient fiction, a kind of mirage, produced by the mind and furnished through cultural forces, but ultimately ephemeral. On the other hand, almost all of us cling desperately to this phantasm, exalt it on the highest pedestal, guard it with militant fervor, and assert its reality through endless Enlightenment-era narratives about "self-realization," "self-help," and "self-discovery." It's a classic "left hand unaware of right hand" dilemma.

Given that sociology has never been too convinced of the reality of the Self and rather unimpressed with its fruit and legacy, it has produced a significant body of literature on the effects of societal and cultural systems built on upon the worship of a mirage. The Yoda version: Veneration of the Self leads to Individualism, Individualism leads to Loss of Community, and Loss of Community leads to Despair. (Or the Dark Side—same thing.)

No sociologist has been more eloquent on this process than Polish analyst Zygmunt Bauman. Modernity, he writes, brings with it as side effect a "compulsive and obligatory self-determination" which is ultimately corrosive for both the individual and society.[18] Persons living in contemporary consumer capitalist societies are immediately confronted with the heavy yoke of autonomy and the terror of endless choices. Pure individualism, he writes, produces pure misery through the incessant expectation of Being Somebody, surrounded by others trying to Be Somebody. Meanwhile, nobody is allowed to be a Nobody. It is a game at the center of which is a trap. To paraphrase Groucho Marx, regardless of who wins the rat race, at the end, you're still a rat.

The trap of individualism at the center of the game called modernity is not merely a philosophical abstraction. It has very tangible and empirical effects on the body and well-being. Epidemiologists are increasingly partnering with social scientists to identify to what extent social and cultural factors contribute to illness, particularly those diseases which have risen dramatically in prevalence in recent decades. Their findings indicate that materialistic and individualistic cultures have higher rates of social isolation, lower self-esteem, higher anxiety, and lower life satisfaction than more collectivist and spiritual cultures. Eckersley concludes:

> The creation of a 'separate self' could be a major dynamic in modern life, impacting on everything from citizenship and social trust, cohesion and engagement, to the intimacy of friendships and the quality of family life. So the issue here is not just a matter of the changed relationship between the individual and society, but of the way in which the individual self is construed. In other words, the result is not only increased objective isolation, but also more subjective loneliness (even in company or within relationships).[19]

The implication of such findings aligns elegantly with a central tenet of sociology: the self was never intended to be a stand-alone entity. Self is only meaningful with and in terms of the other, in this case, community. A culture built wholly on one or the other will be imbalanced, as described by Durkheim nearly a century ago. Eckersley, Bauman, and their chorus trace the core problem to a conflation between autonomy and independence. Though modernity promises and often grants a great deal of the former, particularly though political and legal means, it cannot truly guarantee the latter, since that would be a violation of the fundamental ecological relationship between self and society. Independence, in the final analysis, is impossible, though modern individualistic cultures regularly promote and trumpet it. The only thing possible is a kind of futile narcissism, also predicted by Durkheim. Eckersley summarizes the view nicely: "'Thinking for ourselves' has been redefined as 'thinking of ourselves.'"[20]

* * *

> *"You are a function of what the whole universe is doing in the same way that a wave is a function of what the whole ocean is doing."*
> —*Alan Watts,* The Book: On the Taboo Against Knowing Who You Are

As with many topics we shall investigate in this journey, truths recently discovered by social science are already well-worn assumptions for the ancient spiritual traditions. This is particularly true for the Self. Though the specific treatment may vary a bit by culture and spiritual point of emphasis, the central message is unmistakable: the Self is not the Way. For Western traditions, the Self is to be minimized and put in service of God and others. For Eastern traditions, the Self is an illusion, and service to others is the path to liberation.

There is no evidence that Erving Goffman enjoyed *darshan* with any Hindu gurus, nor any that Mead developed his core ideas after *satori* through Buddhist meditation. Yet both of these architects of the sociological insights about the self display clear parallels with Eastern teaching. Indeed, for Hinduism the self-as-performance idea central to microsociological theory is only the beginning. Not only is the self an elaborate but ultimately unreal production, but so is all of reality. The self, *atman*, is but a personal manifestation of Brahman, the Hindu Ground of all Being. The nature of Brahman, however, is play, which devotees term *lila*. Lila as play has two meanings. It first denotes the literal idea of amusement, pointless enjoyment, as in the kind of play that children instinctively engage in. Brahman enjoys taking the form of endless incarnations, shapes, disguises, and names. There is no big meaning or purpose behind this deific play. It is pure amusement for its own sake. According to Hindu mythology, Brahman hides behinds these masks for a period of eons before gradually revealing himself, destroying the game, and starting over. It is quite literally a cosmic game of hide-and-seek.

The other meaning is obtained directly through the first. As Brahman takes the form of each of us, Brahman is also the director and star of a massive theatrical performance, a play. Birth, growth, joy, suffering, loss, hope, grief, worry, bliss, and even Duck Dynasty—all just part of this epic drama, done for no other reason than lila, joyful play. Thus, the self is profoundly unreal on two levels. Not only is it merely performance without lasting permanence (as in Buddhism), "we" (as individual persons) aren't even the actor behind the mask. It was Brahman all along, the Godhead speaking through, with, and in our every moment. Our *atman*, the ego or self, which feels abundantly real, is actually the temporary local version of Brahman-in-disguise. And so is everyone and everything else. Thus, in this view not believing in God (Brahman) is quite absurd; if one "believes" in reality, one accepts the existence of God as He is hiding behind every facet of it and making each possible. This perspective is not terribly different from Christian theologian Paul Tillich's "Ground of Being," or even St. Paul when he wrote, quoting Epiminedes, "In Him, we live, move, and have our being" (Acts 17:28).[21]

Alan Watts, the most popular Western teacher of Eastern philosophy, once described Buddhism as "Hinduism stripped for export." One readily sees signs of this simplification. Influenced by the dominant Hindic ideas of his native India, Siddhartha Gautama began his investigation of enlightenment through the framework of Brahman, *atman*, and *lila*. However, Siddhartha's technique mercilessly jettisoned any idea for which no evidence or experience could be found. He found the superstructure of Hindu gods, festivals, supernatural action, mythic narratives, and personal devotion unnecessary for liberation and their premises unsupported by his rational inquiries. After his awakening under the Bodhi tree, the Buddha began teaching a path to enlightenment that preserved a number of the core principles of Hinduism minus the cultural and supernatural regalia. Thus, one of the three marks of existence of Buddhism is *anatman*—no self, a deliberate rejection of the Hindu atman.

The doctrine of No Self is one of the most essential and misunderstood ideas in Buddhism. In the West, this doctrine is often thought to mean that Buddhists hold that individuals do not exist, or are unimportant relative to the collective. At other times, it is misinterpreted to mean that personal distinctive-ness and identity should be eradicated. Neither is accurate. *Anatman* merely refers to the lack of evidence for a permanent, unchanging self or essence that is separate and autonomous from everything else. In this way, Buddhism shares an epistemology and conclusions with modern sciences such as sociology and neu-rology. None can find an evidentiary basis for a permanent separate self, though they differ on the implications of that fact. For Buddhism and sociology, both go on to argue that lives built upon the edifice of an illusion are doomed to be unsatisfying.

The Buddhist doctrine of *anatman* further holds that the appearance of self or ego that most of us feel and cling to (another source of suffering according to Buddhism) is actually a product of more fundamental forces called *skand-has*. Skandhas is normally translated as "aggregate" but is more akin to our modern term "composite," meaning a temporary instantiation of component parts. Thus, the self is highly dependent on the functioning of these underlying mechanisms; it has no separate, autonomous existence. Just as the social self is dependent on interactions and the wider community, the ego-mental self relies on other, preexisting faculties. And just as the social self is constantly adapting, changing its performance based on audience feedback, so is the ego-self highly dynamic, subject to changes in its subordinate layers, and lacking any perma-nent features. Buddhism, like sociology, heavily stresses change and is deeply interested in the constancy, power, and mechanisms of change. Accordingly, any notion of self that does not adequately reflect the incessant force of change on all things will be rejected.

Two reactions, not entirely compatible, typically accompany this informa-tion when shared with students. On the one hand, most readily accept the idea that the self is a performance. College students have by this time spent more than a decade perfecting their personae, images, and masks, and are well aware that they are to a large extent, acting. They are also keenly aware that these performances shift from context to context, that they adjust their language, gestures, costumes, and even opinions based on the expected opinion of others. Students often offer vivid stories from their own lives, describing clear instances of face-saving, impression management, and "selves" that were famously ill-suited for their setting. Hilarity ensues. Dramaturgy, it turns out, is fun.

At the same time, however, students find it difficult to accept the deeper meaning of Goffman and Gautama's insight, that the self is essentially empty. Hollow. All hat, no cattle. When asked what they make of all this, and whether they agree, almost all indicate that they cannot accept the idea that they have no essence, no enduring germ of Me-ness that never changes, no matter the context and is immune to social influence. When I ask for evidence, why they believe this, the most common response is, "I just feel it." One particularly plucky Thursday, I countered that perhaps that feeling is also a socialized, downloaded program their mind is running. The only sound in the room was crickets . . . and someone asking Siri: "Google . . . free will. . . ."

It is not easy for young Western minds, growing up in a culture of individualism, pop psychology, and self-realization to grasp the notion of self as illusion. To put it plainly, they don't like the way it makes them feel. And in the United States, emotion will trump evidence every single time.

Thankfully, it is not essential for students to grasp the finer elements of selfology to take away the key message of sociology of the self, nor the spiritual dimensions of the self. Namely, that obsession with the self is, in the famous words of Alan Watts, "an illusion married to a futility." In the spiritual traditions of the West, on the other hand, this futile enterprise is regarded as dangerous, indeed the single greatest blockade to spiritual development and social well-being.

The so-called Abrahamic faiths—Judaism, Christianity, and Islam—share a deep suspicion of the self. Quite distinct from their Eastern counterparts, these traditions acknowledge a more durable ego-self that is the battleground for most spiritual struggles. It is from these ancient religions that modern Westerners inherited the notion of the "split self," "angels and demons," "higher and lower nature," and even the fundamental concept of "original sin." In each case, the ego-self is pitted against another force, often identified as the "will of God," "holiness," or "saintliness."

Judaism holds that humanity was formed with just this type of divided nature. One force, called the *yetzer tov*, which impels us toward the noble, the moral, the Godly, and the *yetzer ra*, which urges us toward the selfish, the hurtful, and the worldly. Torah scholars are quick to point out that both are necessary and the latter one is not inherently evil, but must be balanced and channeled into the best purposes one can find. As a remedy or spiritual practice to minimize the draw of *yetzer ra*, rabbis encourage doing *mitzvah*, or following one of God's commandments. In acting obediently, we undercut our selfish drives and do a thing not because we want to, but because God wants us to. Like Buddhism, much of Judaism is eminently pragmatic.

Islam is also deeply cautious about the ego-self and includes a similar idea about human nature as basically divided into higher and lower forces. In Arabic, "self" and "ego" are roughly translated as *nafs*, which are broken into levels ranging from the lowest and most sinful (the inciting *nafs*) to the most holy (the pure *nafs*). Islam further proscribes several steps to master the *nafs* and elevate followers through the levels, including reflection, resolve, evaluation, conditioning, vigilance, and gratitude. The Prophet Muhammad himself even describes two primary struggles (*jihads*) in life, with the major struggle being the battle with the self, meaning the craving, desirous, harm-inducing portion. The minor struggle is that with external enemies, the version most of us hear about in common usage.

Christianity, the dominant religion of the West, presents an exquisite challenge. If we look to the institutional, doctrinal, and communal Christian tradition that most believers follow, we find a view of the self that is similar in outline to the Jewish notion—fitfully divided between a higher and lower nature—but largely lacking the embrace of the lower ego-self and certainly absent the idea that it has positive value. Instead this sinful nature is precisely the problem and thing to be eradicated. Depending on the theological heritage, this part may be seen as "total depravity" (Calvinist), "brokenness" (evangelical Protestant), or "original sin" (Roman Catholic), among other similar terms. The self is thus a site of constant moral combat, a spiritual battleground between good and evil, (not unlike the Muslim *jihad*) with the evil part generally seen as intrinsic, pre-installed at the factory, as it were.

A number of well-known Bible passages reflect and provide the basis for this concept. Jesus himself describes the process of "dying to self" precisely when he says, "If anyone would come after me, let him deny himself and take up his cross daily and follow me" (Luke 9:23). The Gospels of John and Matthew also provide insight into this view from Jesus with parallel passages: "Whoever loves his life loses it, and whoever hates his life in this world will keep it for eternal life" (John 12:25, Matthew 16:25). Here Jesus is clearly indicating the "self" is the seat of sin and temptation. Clinging to, worshipping, and exalting the self is a path to destruction, both practically and spiritually. In this sense, then, selfishness, ego-centrism, and apathy to others is not a result of evil, it is the root of evil itself. Death to self, as St. Paul writes in many related passages, is the initial and most essential stage in spiritual perfection. For the Christian, this process is epitomized by Jesus himself, whose selflessness extended all the way to the sacrifice of crucifixion.

This is not to say that Christians regard the self as inescapably evil. Indeed, many Bible passages also underscore the intrinsic dignity (the mystics would say "inner divinity") of the individual person. Humans are seen as "made in the image and likeness of God," (Genesis 1:27) "little lower than the angels," (Hebrews 2:9) and so beloved that God sacrificed himself to save them from themselves (John 3:16). But like Buddhists, Muslims, and Jews, Christians are deeply suspicious and cautious of the temptations of the ego-self, all of them acutely aware of its bottomless cravings, impulses, and frequently chaotic nature. It is clear from the Bible and most influential Christian thinkers since that there is little danger if humans becoming excessively altruistic, so committed to the welfare of others that they neglect the self, or even begin to despise the self. The far greater spiritual threat is self-worship, a version of which was the original transgression of Lucifer, for which he was famously exiled from Heaven. Thus, the Christian spiritual path, as with the others, includes innumerable disciplines, texts, rituals, and injunctions that continually pull the follower away from self and toward more durable sources of happiness.

Christian thinkers, like many of their spiritual counterparts from other cultures, also seem to recognize the illusory and deceptive nature of the ego-self, which is now supported by the majority of modern social and natural science. The extraordinary mystical and contemplative tradition of Christianity, exemplified by Meister Eckhart, Teresa of Avila, John of the Cross, Thomas Merton, and more recently Richard Rohr and Simone Weil, has always maintained this position. But they have further argued that the ego-self, if clung to, is actually the greatest barrier to spiritual development and the experience of God. Like social scientists, they hold that is a trap inside a mirage.

Sociologist David Loy summarizes the shared truths of these perspectives beautifully: "The problem and its solution both depend upon the same fact: a constructed sense of self is not a real self. Awakening to our constructedness is the only real solution to our most fundamental anxiety."[22]

CHAPTER THREE

Other

"The fish is in the water, and the water in the fish."
—Arthur Miller

In the mystical branches of spiritual traditions, it is taken for granted that the separation between self and other is unreal. The Hindu *advaita* (nondual) school is the clearest version of this teaching. From the nondual perspective, viewed at the highest possible vantage point (the transcendent, mystical state of consciousness), the entire working of the universe is one enormous continuous process, a single doing. This may be said to be the *sine qua non* sensation of mystical experience, whether it is found in Hindu, Christian, Buddhist, Jewish, or Islamic contexts. It is sought out not only because it is supposedly the real nature of things, untainted by human concepts, but also because it is accompanied by an overpowering feeling of tranquility, joy, and love, according to accounts. As a result, the lives of experiencers are often changed forever, almost always in a positive direction, though their ordinary prior lives are often difficult to rejoin. Transcendent experiences lie at the heart and origin of every major world spiritual tradition. Without them, most major world religions would not have developed or been sustained. Consequently, the entire trajectory of human history has been shaped by these glimpses of a new consciousness and the billions of people inspired by them.

There is something compelling and liberating about the knowledge of fundamental unity. This is likely because it is 100% at odds with our normal socialized way of viewing the world.

From our earliest moments on the planet, we are confronted with the idea of difference. For many of us, our first words are the "proper" names for things and their characteristics. Consider this exchange between my nephew Aaron (age 22 months) and me:

> UNCLE CHRIS: (showing him a picture of a puppy) And what is this?
> AARON: Meow!
> UNCLE CHRIS: Yes, it looks like a kitten, doesn't it? But it's actually a
>   baby dog! What does a dog say?
> AARON: Woof!
> UNCLE CHRIS: Right! So this is a baby dog, called a puppy. What does a
>   baby dog say?
> AARON: (high pitched) woof!
> UNCLE CHRIS: Good! Very good, Aaron! Now what is this? (showing
>   him a squirrel)
> AARON: Meow!

And on it goes

Modern developmental psychologists have established that children under three years of age have a proto-unitary way of experiencing the world (what Freud called "the oceanic feeling") due to their still-forming nervous system. In fact, one of the first (and most jarring) experiences of the first year of life is learning that there is a basic biological boundary between the body and the outside world. This lesson is reinforced through the life course by thousands of experiences of difference.

Socialization instills from a very early age the exact opposite of the nondual perspective. The universe is not a giant single process, we learn, but an infinite number of tiny, mostly unrelated, different things. Sure, some of them are related (trees are more like flowers than cows, for example), but on the whole, it is far from obvious that All is One. This is amplified to an extreme degree, we are taught, when it comes to human beings. After learning we are separate and different from our parents (also not easy), we learn that other humans seem to do what they want. They look different from us. They sound different. As we grow up, we learn that they even perceive the world very differently ("the theory of mind,") and believe things we cannot even understand. By adolescence, we have very little evidence of unity and an ever-growing catalog of diversity. We may even allow this onslaught of difference to make us rather jaded about any hope of lasting harmony and common cause among humanity. That perspective may persist for most of our lives, and affect the actual shape and direction of our biography.

Unless of course, you take a sociology class

Social science, and particularly sociology, is a way of rediscovering this fundamental, forgotten truth. What is lost or buried by years of socialization is found again, but through reason and evidence, and at maturity when it can fully grasped and put into practice. As discussed in the last chapter, the entire idea of Self depends on the Other for its existence and maintenance, a fact revealed in both social science and spiritual traditions. This chapter argues that the reverse is equally true, and examines how recent sociological thinking demonstrates this process. Three themes organize this section: fluidity, interdependence, and pluralism.

Fluidity

Translating from spiritual to sociological terms, we recognize that the Self/Other dichotomy is generally equivalent to "individual" and "society" in the discipline. The relation between these two has launched a thousand articles and books. It is one of the classic puzzles in sociology. Every subfield—family, work, culture, religion, gender, social movements, and deviance to name but a few—daily deal with the dynamic between the individual and society refracted through the specific manifestations of their area. But to truly understand the fundamentals of this important relationship, we must borrow a bit from our cousins in anthropology, whose toolkit is slightly different and often illuminating in such situations.

In 1991, after more than a decade of research, anthropologist Donald Brown itemized in his fascinating *Human Universals* a comprehensive list of characteristics that humans in every part of the globe and time period have displayed.[23] Among the relatively few (about 100) traits, he observed the tendency of humans to form groups with firm boundaries based on the distinction between "us" and "them." This is the beginning of tribal life, and generally the basis of social conflict. It is an outgrowth of the human cognitive inclination toward classification, but applied to other humans, usually initially on the basis of some relatively arbitrary marker, such as skin color, language, or geography.[24,25]

Us/them distinctions are often drawn to enhance survival. If resources are scarce, early humans could only share with those they trusted. Kin are trusted, even if distant, over nonkin (or perceived nonkin). If obvious markers of difference are relatively high, the probability of another group being identified as "them" and even "threatening" is much higher. As Marx pointed out long ago, initial sources of conflict are generally resource-oriented, though with the passage of time, they may be masked by more complex camouflages, such as religion, ideology, race, or simply tradition.[26]

Like all boundaries, especially those of human origin, these ultimately have an unreal or fluid foundation. Across sociology, philosophy, the natural sciences, and especially in spiritual traditions, there is agreement that boundaries are mostly conceptual.[27,28] The tradition of social constructionism since the late 19th century has persuasively argued that many boundary mechanisms used and taken for granted by modern humans are cognitive constructs. Who decides, for example, who is part of "us" and who is "them"? What are the criteria for inclusion? Can the boundary be moved? Is the boundary rigid or permeable? Can one of "them" become one of "us"? How many "thems" are there, after all? None of these are decided by nature. Any boundary, label, category, or behavior connected to them is ultimately decided by human beings, and often for nonrational, even capricious motives.

Abundant illustrations of the validity of this view are provided by everyday life. Students often tell me of attending out-of-town football games and having to sit in or near the home bleachers. Inevitably, this results feelings of awkwardness, alienation, even hostility. After all, "we" are "mixing" with them. Neither party is happy about it. Dirty glances, mild taunting, and even creating distance is common. Occasionally one or a few students will comprise the actual boundary between their team and our team, often denoted by colors. For those border students, strange things often occur. If conversation opens up, students on either side of the border may accidentally discover they attended the same high school. Or both love Taylor Swift. Or share a mutual friend. Or are both Methodist. A few even find out that they are distantly related. What happens next is priceless.

Without fail, both students will nearly forget about their previous animosity and discomfort. What is shared overwhelms what separates them. They may even tell the friends they came with that this new person is "one of us now" or "is not so bad after all." The boundary has opened up to welcome them. In some cases it disappears altogether.

The boundary between "us" and "them" is constructed, permeable, portable, and arbitrary. But, and this is important, they are real. How are they real? In short, because we have decided they are. Social constructionists, such as those cited above, are likewise clear on this issue. Regardless of their ultimate ontological emptiness, they have real effects, real uses, and are recognized as real by a great many people. Recognizing that the boundary between Mexico and the U.S. is constructed makes little difference in the pragmatic realities of immigration. Knowing that the differences between the Central and Pacific time zones are entirely artificial will not help me make my flight. Similar examples from ordinarily life are countless.

The Hindu *advaita* tradition has a useful way of thinking about these discrepant truths by dividing reality into levels. The level where humans mainly carry out their affairs is known as the Relative realm, where differences are recognized as real and have tangible consequences. But below that is the realm of the Absolute, where these boundaries and distinctions fall away, and all things are revealed as interconnected and part of a seamless whole. Likewise, the sociological perspective known as critical realism also views reality as stratified, consisting of Objective Reality (akin to the Absolute), the Actual (between Absolute and Relative, where causation occurs), and the Empirical (equivalent to the Relative) where events can be measured and named. According to critical realism, science (including sociology) mostly is restricted to the Empirical, but makes inferences about the Actual through its observations about causal mechanisms.[29,30] Most humans have little to no contact with the Absolute/Objective, though the mystical traditions provide a regular mode of access.

Interdependence

Since the boundaries and distinctions we draw are ultimately without Absolute Reality, but make plenty of Empirical Difference, then it stands to reason that entities on both sides of the boundaries—"us/them," "self/other," or "subject/object"—are actually merely different aspects of the same thing. Neither is more necessary or superior to the other. In fact, it is becoming increasingly clear that these different manifestations mutually imply each other and generally need each other. It was shown in the last chapter, for example, that sociology and spiritual traditions agree that the Self is impossible without society, that the "self" is almost entirely a social product. But it turns out the reverse is also true, that the self also shapes society. The result is a web of interdependence, a pattern that will be familiar to any practitioner of spirituality.

The issue of understanding the relationship between individual and society is generally referred to in sociology as the "structure/agency" debate. It is also perhaps the slipperiest and most difficult problem in the field. Until the 1970s, sociologists mostly held the position that individuals were greatly overpowered by social forces, with some, such as Parsons, even contending that the individual was a mere "imprint" or "product" of their surrounding social and cultural structure. Marxists, Durkheimians, and even most Weberian social analysts were largely in agreement, though they disagreed about the specific piece of society that was most influential. For Marxists, it was the economy; for Durkheimians, it was culture; and for Weberians, it was power, usually political. The explosion of social movements, cultural innovations, and political revolutions that rocked the 1960s and 1970s left "strong structure" sociologists such as these with much to answer for. How was so much social change possible? Why was so much of it in a radical (anticapitalist, grassroots, counterdominant) direction? How were ordinary, nonelite individuals able to overcome such long-standing structures with few advantages on their side?

Without satisfactory explanations to contribute, both students and practicing social scientists of the "strong structure" camp searched for alternative traditions or tools. Parsonian functionalism was largely abandoned. Durkheim was relegated to "classical" (i.e. "obsolete") theory. Marxist theory was deeply retooled to consider culture more seriously and the agency of the masses. In a phrase, structure was out; agency and culture were in.

The "cultural turn," as it was later dubbed, had an influential and fascinating run through the 1980s and 1990s. Led by British cultural studies, including scholars such as Stuart Hall, Raymond Williams, and Terry Eagleton, sociology began to borrow and lend theory with literary criticism, postmodern philosophy, and communication studies. At the same time in the United States, a focus on meaning-making, interactions, and qualitative methods was filling the void left by the macrostructuralists. Harold Garfinkel, Erving Goffman, and Sheldon Stryker gained prominence and influence through this period, elaborating sophisticated methods and theories for studying and understanding the micro-level of social life. In this perspective, the individual agent is knowledgeable, strategic, and sensitive to feedback (reflexive), in almost perfect contrast to the individual in structural sociology. Symbolic interactionists such as these scholars did not refute the power of culture, economics, or politics to influence the behavior and beliefs of individuals. They merely observed that these influences were not passively received. Instead, agents used creativity to "mobilize" cultural forms, economic realities, and political forces in unexpected ways. Such innovations were responsible, ultimately, for social change, both in mundane and sometimes revolutionary ways. The groundwork laid by microsociologists made possible much more satisfactory explanations of the types of social movements seen in the 1960s and 1970s, work led by David Snow, Alberto Melucci, Doug McAdam, and William Gamson.

Since the 1990s, the search for a realistic and satisfactory middle way between structure and agency has been pursued in earnest in social science. Two efforts stand out: the structuration theory of Anthony Giddens, and the critical realist approach of Margaret Archer.[31,32] A detailed discussion of each is impossible here, but we can point up a few of their key agreements and differences.

Giddens and Archer agree that agents and structures depend upon one another. Individuals create and maintain social systems through their repeated practices, called structuration by Giddens and the ungainly "morphostasis" by Archer. They also agree that social change can occur when resources or meanings are modified at either level. Same-sex marriage, for example, is increasingly common in the U.S. because of changes at the legal and political level, allowing more gay and lesbian couples to join the institution of marriage. In part, these institutional changes are the result of shifting cultural attitudes. However, it is also the case that these legal changes have shifted public opinion. Which is the real cause? Structure/agency is the sociological equivalent of the chicken/egg problem. Giddens and Archer fortunately agree that both occur and equally necessary.

Where they mainly disagree, interestingly, is regarding time. For Archer, structure always precedes the individual in time; the agent is born into a pre-established social structure, no matter how primitive. Structuration denies primacy to either structure or agency, which Archer cannot abide.

How could such dry and abstract social theory produce inspiration? Can Giddens and Archer give rise to epiphanies and mystical insight? Surely I'm not suggesting that the Gospel of Structuration can liberate me? Or that the Noble Critical Realist Path is the way to bliss?

Not quite. But it will definitely help

If Giddens, Archer, and their many interpreters are right, we should be immensely happy and relieved. There is indeed Good News here. And it is same good news carried by the world's spiritual traditions for centuries. That message is twofold and quite simple: we are all connected, and we can change the world.

Both perspectives stress that the self and the society are inextricably bound together. We individuals, through our practices and interactions, actually create society. The social world is a product of our action. At the same time, that society is the primary force in shaping the Self, as detailed in the last chapter. Thus, if we desire change in either, we can begin with either or both. Outraged about sweatshop labor? Stop purchasing from merchants who profit from such conditions (individual level) Or join a campaign to make such practices illegal (societal). Concerned about the quality of education in the U.S.? Become a mentor or tutor in a struggling local school (individual). Or make sure your tax dollars support the schools that most need the revenue by choosing to live near such schools (meso-level). Or run for office on a platform of educational equality (societal). Every social problem, according to structure-agency theorists, is open to exactly this type of change. Thanks to sociology, we can not only see precisely how large scale structural challenges begin and are maintained by individual action, but we can also better target solutions to these problems by aiming them at both levels. Most politicians and activists would have us focus on one or the other, with conservatives typically stressing individual action (or none at all, depending on the issue) and progressives almost always pointing to enormous policy level interventions. Giddens himself, acting as consultant to former President Clinton and former British Prime Minister Tony Blair, has pushed for the necessity of attacking social problems at the collective and personal levels, an approach he calls "Third Way politics," the third way between two extremes.

Social theory, it turns out, is not just fascinating, but incredibly practical.

The tight web of interdependence woven between the self and society is nothing new to spirituality. In the Eastern traditions, the parable of the Web of Indra provides a beautiful and fitting description. Originally imagined as the net of Indra, a deity of the Hindu Vedas, the web is unique because of its structure. At the vertex of each web strand lies a jewel with many faces. In each facet of the jewel, one can see the reflection of all other jewels, and naturally that jewel is likewise reflected in all the others. Each thus "contains" and displays all the others, similar to fractal geometry. The individual is a microcosm of the whole, and the whole is a macrocosm of the one. Pulitzer Prize-winning cognitive scientist Douglas Hofstadter applies the image of Indra's web to social science to describe the inherent interdependency of social networks, which is quickly becoming the dominant metaphor and framework for sociology.[33] Social networks are the infrastructure for all social orders.

Western spiritual and religious traditions are no stranger to the ideas of interdependence and emergence. The entire notion of evangelization is premised on

changing individuals. Without this degree of agency and freedom from structural dominance, evangelism and indeed even secular paths of transformation
such as Alcoholics Anonymous would be meaningless and futile. But within
evangelism, the change that often occurs within the individual is not intended
solely for the individual. That inner change is designed to bring about external changes in the broader world—the original meaning of the word "repent."
Observable differences in behavior and relations with others, presumably in
a loving and kind direction, are the objective. Since self and other are deeply
intertwined and ultimately inseparable, any change the individual makes will
have effects on the broader web of society. The size of the worldly change will
depend on the scope of the individual change and the reach of their network,
but it never stops with the self. The very structure of the human ecosystem
prohibits it.

This is the deeper meaning and origin of the Golden Rule, often attributed
to Christianity but found within all ancient spiritual traditions. "Do to others
as you would have them do to you" is not simply an ethical proscription. It is
a statement about the real nature of things. A more precise wording might be
"Your action upon others *is* action upon yourself." Jesus himself identifies with
this radical repositioning of Self when he says "Whenever you have done this to
the least of them, you have done it to me" (Matthew 25:45).

Another tradition within Christianity takes a slightly different view on
interdependence and emergence. The Social Gospel movement began in the late
19th century through the thinking and writing of iconoclasts such Josiah Strong,
Walter Rauschenbusch, and Washington Gladden. The premise was simple: the
"Kingdom of God" referenced so often in the New Testament refers not to an
afterlife paradise accessible through spiritual salvation, *but this world, here and
now.* A primary mission of Jesus, therefore, was to show followers how to create
a new social order, one that is in line with God's original design and intention
for the Earth. Sin, therefore, was not mainly a personal, interior problem that
could be reconciled through piety and individual repentance. Instead—and
this was revolutionary—sin was social, systemic, and institutional. Rauschenbusch, steeped through his studies in Germany in Marxist analysis, asserted
that immoral practices could also be rooted in giant impersonal structures that

preceded the individual in time (a la Archer above) and survived the person's lifetime. Thus, all the individual confession and salvation in the world would not be sufficient to resolve modern challenges such as ecological damage, predatory lending, educational inequality, and human rights abuses without focusing effort at the macroinstitutional level.

Whereas conventional evangelicals would likely also work toward the eradication of such evils, their tactics would differ, focusing instead on changing the hearts and minds of individual sinners. Through their interior transformation, they would then repent of any such violations themselves, and then see to the conversion of others in like fashion. For Social Gospellers, this method works, but is unacceptably slow and inadequate to the task. In sociological terms, they would say it is too interactionist and naïve of structuration to be effective. The Social Gospel movement, deeply influenced by the social science of its time, was still visionary in this respect, pioneering a theory of emergence and a praxis of social change built on ideas that would not be mainstream in sociology for another 60 years. The weakness of the Social Gospel approach, famously publicized by a fundamentalist backlash in the 1920s, was its neglect of the individual and her spiritual well-being, a cornerstone of Christian belief. This neglect was powerfully overcome by the late 20th century, when a deeply privatized, charismatic and intimacy-based Christianity rose to popularity, led by a move to nondenominational and Bible-based churches. Nevertheless, the legacy of Social Gospel theology and practice remains through dozens of federal social programs, such as the New Deal, Medicare, as well as labor unions.

Self and society, though always interdependent, were forever changed by modernity around the time of the Industrial Revolution. Modernity is that slippery concept that everyone seems to use but no one knows how to define. Sociology has been called the "science of modernity," and although that is a bit confining, it is not entirely wrong. Founding sociologists such as Marx and Durkheim argued that modern processes fundamentally reshaped human life forever. Primary among these was a beautiful paradox, described by both: Modernity ironically made both individualism and interdependence stronger. What does that mean?

Durkheim noted that as societies grow in size and complexity, they special-
ize, much like organisms. As sectors of the society dedicate their efforts to one
rather than several functions, they become highly dependent on each other for
overall survival. Yet simultaneously, the growing society was also more prone
to factionalization if they did not share a sufficient amount of similarity and a
common sense of the "sacred." Modern societies also typically embrace science,
the rights of the individual, and democracy. Thus, economic interdependency
increases while the drive for individual autonomy rises as well. This results in
tighter bonds of *exchange*, which are typically impersonal, and looser bonds
of *community*, which are personal and voluntary. These latter bonds, as noted
above, maintain healthy levels of connection between self and society, pro-
tecting against pathology at either level. Durkheim predicted (correctly) that
the replacement of community with exchange would produce unprecedented
degrees of *anomie*, a feeling of emptiness, loss of meaning, and absence of direction. Individualism plus greater interdependence can equal misery.

Marx, too, was driven by a desire to combat the alienation produced by
modernity; indeed it was the original motive for all his economic and phil-
osophic work. For Marx, alienation was the result of modernity only insofar
as capitalism was a part of modernity. Capitalism, which he argued was based
on exploitation, dehumanization, and efficiency, naturally generated a loss of
connection and dignity. The masses, he contended, would bear the brunt of
alienation, but even elites and owners would be degraded through their objectification of others and rampant materialism. The global techno-capitalism of
the 21st century is a perfect illustration of Marx's concerns and predictions,
with entire nations constituting the labor force for other countries.[34] Workers in
Bangladesh or Mexico have no chance of ever owning or consuming the products they make, nor meeting the owners of their factories, and certainly never
knowing those who buy their handiwork. This is precision, scientific alienation.
And yet "core" countries such as the U.S. and Europe are entirely dependent on
these workers for their daily luxuries at everyday low prices. Furthermore, the
unrivaled affluence, freedom, and individualism of the West have not produced
a loving, warm utopia. The alienation and anomie described by these sociologists is the spiritual blight of our time.

Concerned observers from the worlds of spirituality and social science have naturally come forth with diagnoses and prescriptions. Their recommendations are remarkably similar. Sociologists such as Robert Bellah and Amitai Etzioni, representing the "communitarian" perspective have written persuasively for decades about the need to repair the bonds of emotional, social, and cultural connection damaged by modernity and individualism. Central to their analyses is the privileging of the Self over the Other, reinforced with a conviction that the Other really is Other, in a threatening sense. Competition has replaced cooperation, the private has retreated from the public, and the social is a thing to be used rather than a place to belong. Communitarians also point out that such views are based on a fundamental mistake: that the Self exists and society does not (paraphrasing Margaret Thatcher).[35] Consequently, the problems of the self—anomie and alienation—cannot be healed except by nurturing both self and society.

Probably the most consistent modern voice on the tight link between personal and collective well-being is His Holiness the 14th Dalai Lama. Consider his words on "Ethics for the New Millennium":

> We come into the world as the result of others' actions. We survive here in dependence on others.... For this reason it is hardly surprising that most of our happiness arises in the context of our relationships with others. Nor is it so remarkable that our greatest joy should come when we are motivated by concern for others. But that is not all. We find that not only do altruistic actions bring about happiness but they also lessen our experience of suffering.... What does this tell us? Firstly, because our every action has a universal dimension, a potential impact on others' happiness, ethics are necessary as a means to ensure that we do not harm others. Secondly, it tells us that genuine happiness consists in those spiritual qualities of love, compassion, patience, tolerance and forgiveness and so on. For it is these which provide both for our happiness and others' happiness.[36]

His words resonate with the recent admonition from Pope Francis on the dangers amidst the promise of modernity. "New ideologies, characterized by rampant individualism, egocentrism and materialistic consumerism, weaken social bonds," he wrote, "fuelling that 'throw away' mentality which leads to contempt for, and the abandonment of, the weakest and those considered 'useless.' "[37]

Sociology and spirituality are beginning to speak in harmony, though through different registers, on the simple truth that Self and Other are one system, one living organism. As a student once summarized in an essay at the end of the term, "If you want to be happy, help someone else be happy. If you really want to help others, begin by loving yourself."

Pluralism: The Challenge of the Other

Each semester since 2011, I have taught a course for seniors majoring in sociology. This "Capstone" course (officially known as "Senior Colloquium") is standard fare at many U.S. liberal arts universities, and is designed to provide a summary and review of the sociological lessons hopefully gained along the last four years. It is also intended to sharpen and refine essential social science research skills, mainly achieved through a longish proposal for original research, which goes through several drafts and revisions. But because such a course would be dreadfully dull if solely comprised of technical enhancement, I also assign several topical books to provide a secondary curriculum on current social quandaries. The books reflect both my personal and academic interests: morality, culture, politics, media, inequality, and policy-making. For years, though, I struggled internally with a thread or motif that encapsulated all of these seemingly varied subjects. It was not an urgent or significant problem, but irritating to be sure. At the conclusion of one particularly rewarding semester, I got the gumption to ask the class what one theme best summarized our readings. Without hesitation, an unusually gifted student (who went on to graduate studies at Duke Divinity School) replied, "Dealing with difference."

My mouth fell open; I shook my head, and grinned.
"Thank you. That's exactly right."

Though I could not see it at the time—a classic case of missing the forest for the trees—my students had picked up on the essential message of the course.

Upon reflection, it struck me that "dealing with difference" (properly known as "pluralism" in sociology) was more than my pet lesson; it is one of the core challenges in sociology as a whole. Moreover, pluralism is arguably the most imperative issue facing modern societies, particularly the practical matter of maintaining social harmony amidst unprecedented diversity.

On one level, pluralism is nothing new. Humans have always been diverse. We have always disagreed. Conflict is more or less a constant. And crucially, we have found nonviolent ways through it. Coexistence is at least as much a part of human history as is division and warfare, and peaceful pluralism, according to Steven Pinker, has never been more widespread than in the modern era.[38] Paradoxically, the collision of ideologies and civilizations brought about by modernity has also made mass violence and devastating conflict less likely. Globalization, which has brought societies into regular contact which only a century ago would have never heard of each other, affords opportunities for both turmoil (such as the U.S. and North Korea) and also historic alliances (such as E.U. support for Burmese independence). Regardless of its outcomes, scholars agree that contemporary pluralism is distinct in a few ways. First, in terms of degree, 21st century pluralism is faster and broader than in previous eras. In 1915, for an American farmer to have a conversation about religion or food with an Indian banker required either nearly impossible technical feats of telegraphy or several train and ocean liner journeys. In 2015, it occurs hundreds of times per week in mere seconds thanks to advances in both communication and transportation. In 1915, the typical American rarely left her hometown and the most unusual person she would meet might be an African-American or migrant worker. In 2015, the typical kindergartner will encounter more diversity than that by recess.

Second, the explosion of diversity has been in type as well as quantity. Twenty-first century social life includes an ever-growing spectrum of ways of being human. Identity in the age of the Internet is as customizable as the video games and computers we use. Shall I get a neck tattoo or feathers attached to my cervical spine? Should I be vegan, lacto-vegetarian, paleo, or gluten free? Are my politics Tea Party, Green Party, Anarcho-Syndicalist, or Neo-Liberal? Can I get away with calling myself a Hin-Jew (Hindu and Jewish)? What about a

EpiscoBuddhist? Will I be able to get along with my coworker who is Agnosti-farian or my boss who loves Oprah and Joel Osteen (an OpSteen?) Ugh. Plu-ralism is exhausting.

If Pinker is right and conflict has become less lethal in the modern era, it may be because, in part, warfare has been replaced by "Operations," and Evil Empires by rogue states and terrorist cells. Perhaps the scale of fighting and bloodshed has shrunk, but in its place is a greater number of low-grade, sim-mering, and seemingly intractable conflicts. The character of conflict itself has changed as well. Major battles over territory, resources, or nationalism are rarer, while skirmishes over language, religion, ideology and other identity markers are more common. Even before shots are fired and words give way to violence, lesser but still significant "culture wars" engulf entire populations and test the bounds of the social order. These are particularly common in the unprecedented number of liberal democracies in the modern world.

The United States is especially prone to pluralistic challenges given its many overlapping subcultures, freedom of expression, and value of equality. Within the U.S., the challenge of the Other manifests as residential resegregation, debates over same-sex marriage, immigrant rights, treatment of the mentally ill, political polarization, and most visibly, in interfaith relations. Those who struggle most mightily in such arenas are the groups that take issue with the very existence of pluralism itself. For these purists (frequently fundamental-ists and related antimodernists), only the elimination of choice, diversity, and mixing will bring social harmony. In contrast to the spiritual disciplines within them, religions have often seen society not as an extension of the self or the natural environment for human flourishing, but instead as a contaminating force. Religious groups at "high tension" with the temporal realm are promi-nent in this regard.[39] Many have gone to extraordinary lengths to avoid contact with "the world," including developing entire retreatist communities, parallel institutions, and subcultural identities. Their fears are not unfounded. Since the advent of modernity, the stakes for religion could not be higher. The ways of knowing, behaving, and believing are all fundamentally threatened by the premises of modernity, at least in principle. Pluralism, say such groups, must go away.

Pluralism is not going away. On this, almost all social scientists, spiritual traditions, and serious observers of human relations agree. And, more to the point, it should not. Pluralism, for lack of a better term, is good. The ancient wisdom traditions, particularly the Eastern variants, would even assert that it is natural and indeed, unavoidable. Hsin Hsin Ming, the revered Zen master, spoke to this question when he said, "In the landscape of spring, there is neither better nor worse. The flowering branches grow naturally, some long, some short."[40] From a strictly evolutionary perspective, humanity is diverse because heterogeneity produces more strong offspring than homogeneity. The dizzying collision of human differences born of modernity is a challenging miracle, a terrifying masterpiece, a gorgeous chaos.

Indeed, in the absence of pluralism, sociology finds little reason to be. The field, after all, is based on the study of variation. Variables are our bread and butter. Pluralism has given sociology, and all social sciences, a near infinite array of subjects, perspectives, interpretations, and directions. What does sociology have to offer in return? The answer is twofold, and if engaged with diligence, is indeed a spiritual practice.

First, sociology can serve as a social diagnostician. In the same way that a physician orders a series of tests to ascertain a patient's health status, sociologists use their instruments to assess the wellness of society. While a medical doctor may use MRI scans, blood assays, and their clinical exam to measure a patient's well-being, comparing them against normal ranges and signs, sociologists employ population surveys, in-depth interviews, and group observation to identify and describe how healthy the social body is. Of key utility for a clinician is the medical history or chart, which describes the patient's prior illnesses, conditions, treatments, and genetic predispositions. Likewise, the sociologist will consult a society's recent and distant history, examine its cultural heritage, and become familiar with its tendencies and past policies. They will also, like a physician, compare the society or culture with other similar or thriving ones to determine a rough sense of its overall condition and challenges.

Governments actually use sociology in this way all the time. The Census, for example, is the most accurate and comprehensive description of U.S. society, and is essentially a group of social scientists who work for the federal government rather than a university. A number of other large and famous social surveys have a tacit but unmistakable interest in the health of society, sometimes literally. Why else would the General Social Survey now be linked to the National Death Index if sociologists were not interested in the social causes of mortality and longevity? Would the National Longitudinal Study of Adolescent to Adult Health (Add Health) survey even exist if sociologists and citizens were not concerned about the well-being of young people? Through such measurements, societies obtain a trustworthy dashboard of their political, cultural, and economic vitality, the challenges they face or will face, as well as the progress and triumphs they have achieved. No other social institution is equipped for such a task.

Second, sociology can guide humanity in how to build and maintain community. Armed with the information provided through rigorous data collection, sociologists can then make evidence-based recommendations for how to cope with, resolve, or heal the social order. Just as we do not ask physicians to merely diagnose our health problems but also to remedy them, sociologists can and do provide prescriptions for overcoming social problems. In order to do this, we must embrace the spiritual and normative identity of sociology, present at its origins and if we are honest, barely under the surface in its contemporary form. In the case of pluralism, sociology is uniquely appropriate to the challenge. Revisiting arguments made above, we can affirm both empirically and theoretically, that ultimately, self and other are merely arbitrary divisions. Whatever we believe divides you and I through difference is overwhelmed by the amount we share as members of the human family. Supported by state of the art social theory, we can stress that those with whom we differ we also profoundly depend upon, and they upon us, bound up as we inevitably are in the web of interconnection. We can argue too that differences need not be a basis for conflict, that this is merely a choice, and that difference can instead be a basis for learning and fascination, buttressed by research from network, urban, and social movement sociologists.

Most importantly, since Durkheim's seminal formulation of solidarity, the field has been deeply attentive to the factors that produce functional, stable, and positive social orders. In that spirit, sociology has amassed an unrivaled "recipe book" for community building. For example, it is well established that regular, face-to-face contact with neighbors strengthens commitment to the community and prevents crime. Such engagements have also been shown to decrease racial and ethnic hostility and increase feelings of tolerance.[41,42] It is no coincidence that Dr. Martin Luther King, Jr., who earned his bachelor of arts in sociology, named his clearest vision for the future of America the "beloved community." At the heart of every sociologist's work, I believe, is a similar utopian motive.

Finally, the sociological worldview itself, steeped as it is in values of cultural relativism, bracketing of personal values, and curiosity toward human variation, brings an inherently open mind toward the Other. By simply studying and internalizing the way sociologists see the world, such as through taking introductory courses, reading key sociological works, or doing a bit of hands-on research, the odds of success in "dealing with difference" are vastly improved. In so doing, it becomes clear that sociology is a spiritual *practice*, rather than mere dogma.

In Southern Africa, the Nguni Banti language has a term that perfectly expresses the spiritual perspective on pluralism and the Other: *Ubuntu*. English has no exact single word counterpart for the term, but it is often translated as "I am because we are." Another elaboration is "A person is a person through other people." Resembling the previous idea of interdependence between self and society, *ubuntu* also communicates an expectation of warmth, hospitality, and acceptance toward strangers (the Other). For those embracing *ubuntu*, the Other is none other than myself, and I have an innate interest in being kind to myself. Pluralism and its identity-based conflicts under *ubuntu* is both a declaration of the real nature of humanity, worthy of rejoicing in, and a basis for dialing down the intensity of tension and attachment to identities. We are more inclined to see ourselves in the eyes of the stranger, the outcast, and the enemy. We owe "them" for helping "us" to exist at all. Thus, my hostility or avoidance of the other should be replaced with gratitude and openness.

The philosophy of *ubuntu* had no contact with Western social science, but the parallels are strikingly apparent. Both are tapping into a core truth about human nature and social life that belongs to no single tradition. Ubuntu shares ethical and philosophical traits with almost the entirety of the Easter spiritual traditions, most of whom regard difference as a manifestation of the nature of Divinity itself and thus sacred. Christian Trappist Monk and mystic Thomas Merton wrote a number of essays and letters expressing similar sentiments of unity and joy in diversity. In a letter to Dorothy Day, founder of the Catholic Worker, he said: "

> It is when we love the other, the enemy, that we obtain from God the key to an understanding of who he is, and who we are...To shut out the person and to refuse to consider him as a person, as an other self, we resort to the impersonal "law" and to abstract "nature." And we justify the evil we do to our brother because he is no longer a brother, he is merely an adversary, an accused...Instead of pushing him down, trying to climb out by using his head as a stepping-stone for ourselves, we help ourselves to rise by helping him to rise."[43]

Because of this, society is seen by some religious traditions and disciplines as *the* site of spiritual practice. Through service, promotion of social justice, and community, followers live out the sacred values of their faith and express their devotion to the Divine. Within the major branches of Judaism, Islam, Christianity, Buddhism, and Hinduism, the protection and service of the human family is a constitutive part of faithful living, not an option or hobby.

Whether we take the empirical, sociological path or the *ubuntu*-style, spiritual path, we end up at the same destination and learn many of the same lessons. The challenge of the Other is only as real as long as we uphold the reality of the Other. Seeing sociologically we understand the causes and effects of viewing the Other as truly separate or threatening, and respond with intelligence and fairness. Seeing spiritually we recognize the original connection between all human beings, and respond with love and service.

CHAPTER FOUR

Truth

"Learn what is true in order to do what is right."
—*Thomas Huxley*

"The truth will set you free, but first it will make you miserable."
—*James A. Garfield*

In 2005, comedian Stephen Cochaplbert introduced the world to a much-needed term: "truthiness." According to Colbert, truthiness is marked not by the veracity of a claim, but the emotional certainty with which it is held. "It's not just that I feel it to be true, it's that *I* feel it to be true. There's an air of self-importance about it," he added.[44] Truthiness, said Colbert, is a concept custom-made for the 21st century, which he argued, stresses not what is, but what we want to be. Evidence, facts, and logic are the currency of a bygone era. Perception, opinion, and feeling are the coin of the realm in the age of the iPhone. And news provided by Comedy Central.

Colbert's point, however, is far more profound than we initially recognize. Truthiness would have no truck today if it did not resonate with a vaster current of philosophical and moral developments circulating through culture for a long time. Without putting too fine a point on it, truth—and especially Truth—is passé. Though the Enlightenment and modern science put truth at the core of its enterprise and fought hard to prove and publicize it, intellectual trends since the mid-20th century have made even talking about truth seem a silly and futile effort. Every field of inquiry has seen its version of this transition. In physics, it was the move from the rigid laws and objects of Newton to the squishy and contingent quantum world of Bohr and Planck. In philosophy, it was the transformation of Locke and Hume's empiricism into the "truth regimes" of Foucault and Derrida via postmodernism. In sociology, it has largely been versions of postmodernism, such as constructionism and a forceful critique of variable-based sociology. The common element across each is a deep suspicion of the static, objective nature of reality, knowledge, and ways of knowing. The effects have been far-reaching for these fields, and for humanity as a whole.

To be clear, the argument is not that truth is dead, or unreal, or even worthless to pursue. Instead, it is a more subtle claim that truth is always and everywhere contextualized. That is, what is seen or defined as true in any given time or place is a product of that time and place. Truth is not timeless, unchanging, absolute, or universal. Truth, even for physicists and philosophers, is a construct of those who are observing the phenomena. As such, "the truth" is a kind of Rorschach blot, telling us at least as much about the observers as it does about the event. Truth is thus a profoundly human, social process.

As mentioned in Chapter 3, the field of critical realism, similar to Eastern philosophy, holds that reality is stratified and that we as human observers only have access to those aspects which manifest as either events (the actual, those inferred) or as observations (the empirical, those measured). The level beneath this, the Real, is beyond human apprehension and access. This level contains, theoretically, many True, Real structures which are effectively absolute, universal, and require no human interaction. Strict empiricists, such as the majority of intellectuals until the mid-20th century, held that Truth and the Observed were equivalent. All that was meaningfully true was measurable. If it did not register as data, or it lacked evidence of a humanly graspable sort, it was not true.

For spiritual traditions, this brand of rock-ribbed empiricism has proved to be a force of destruction. Every manner of supernatural claim made by spiritual people is rejected or explained away by this aggressive scientism. Since the early 2000s, the fashionable version of this has been use of neuroscience to erase the distinctiveness of spiritual experiences (Harris, Newberg, etc.). Since the "soul" or "spirit" do not appear on fMRI scanners or EEGs, medical empiricism cannot accept their existence. They might be real, but there is no evidence of them. Therefore, the "*unio mystica*" of the Catholic nun, the *satori* of the Zen meditator, the precognitive knowledge of the Kabbalist, and the ecstasy of the whirling dervish are all merely perturbations of neural chemistry. Knowing "how it works" is apparently the same as knowing "what it is." And knowing "what it means" or "how it affects people" is unimportant. It is possible, of course, that St. Paul experienced a temporal lobe seizure on the road to Damascus, but not everyone that has epilepsy starts a global religion. Pure empiricism has no explanation for this result, and no interest in pursuing it, apparently.

Against this stern black-and-white world come the interpretativists, building off the postmodern movement in philosophy which reemphasized the power of subjectivity in all inquiry. What is also present at the moment of measurement? You! Who decides what is counted and what is not? You! Who chose this research question and not another? You! And if not you per se, then some other You, or a group of Yous called a social order. And social orders always organize around power, status, resources, and ideology. Facts, data, variables, and reason, to paraphrase Kant, are always the effects of passions, morals, biases, and power. The very fact that we call this type of person "black" and another "white" reflects a preexisting system of categories that we did not have the power to create. We work within that regime of discourse, Foucault would say, and it structures our thinking and measurement in incalculable ways with tremendous effects. Truth is not out there, as "The X-Files" would have us believe. It's in here (in us.)

During the 1980s and 1990s, a dramatic intellectual war waged between these two camps, and we still live with the effects of it today in science and politics. But in large measure, both the modern and postmodern sides have been overwhelmed by a new and unforeseen enemy. This foe has devastated the idea of truth in far more consequential ways. For this force is not caught up in the battle saying "There is truth," or "There is no truth." It simply intimates—"Truth is irrelevant."

A growing body of social observers are pointing out that since the advent of the Internet, social media, and smartphones, something like truthiness is more important than truth.[45] This transformation was presciently described by Aldous Huxley a half-century ago in *Brave New World Revisited*, in which he noted humanity's "insatiable appetite for distraction."[46] He predicted that future dictatorships would not have to resort to violence and terror to maintain power, but merely provide endless varieties of pleasure to lull the population into a passive, pleasant prison of their design.

iCulture, as this technologized mental environment has been called, is characterized by immediacy, customization, choice, and contagion. At the center of iCulture is the individual, namely, the Ego. The Internet exists, according to the values of iCulture, for the indulgence and exploration of the Self. As a result, every app, news feed, subscription, and setting is customized to the preferences of the individual. Information, experiences, and relationships that are not to the liking of the Self are jettisoned, blocked, or never even seen. In many cases, technology and its digital realities are sought precisely to avoid real, flesh-and-blood experiences that may be unpleasant. The First Commandment of iCulture is clear: Me and My Pleasure are sacred.

Feelings in iCulture are paramount. Emotions largely take the place of values and evidence in this landscape. But not all feelings are equal. Emotions such as shame, fear, sadness, and contentment have virtually no place and no value here. The greatest horror is FOMO, or the dreaded Fear of Missing Out.[47] The most treasured feeling is pleasure (distinct from happiness), and the best form of pleasure is novelty. The ideal form of novel pleasure is flattery. Ergo: Bliss = 100 new Likes or re-Tweets of the picture of my new haircut in less than five minutes. In the words of the immortal grunge band, Temple of the Dog, "Say hello to heaven."

Such an arrangement is not hospitable to truth. Truth has a famously irritating way of being boring. Truth is also frequently not about me, not new, and not pleasurable. Most problematic is that truth requires work. The search for truth is often a painstaking, tedious, frustrating, and unrewarding process. Many who seek truth are punished (e.g. Galileo, MLK, Edward Snowden) and the truth they reveal rarely results in higher status or wealth. In a phrase, truth doesn't make me feel good. Therefore…back to Candy Crush.

In a world where one can choose between iCulture and Old Culture (perhaps better called Us Culture), the reasons to choose the latter are not obvious or appealing. Old Culture requires conversation, listening, waiting, tolerance, participation, creativity, and, again, effort. It also involves two often-overlooked social ingredients: empathy and responsibility. In order to feel empathy and responsibility, I have to first decenter my universe from Self, which is both uncomfortable and of questionable pay-off. Supposing I successfully recalibrate my reality with Us or The Community as the center, I am then confronted with the unpleasant and sometimes overwhelming problem of having feelings about someone other than myself. Blargh. What's the point? This cat on YouTube is riding a Roomba with a shark mask and chasing a baby! Dat's on fleek AF!

iCulture is bringing about a profound shift in consciousness. Within iCulture, the events that pop up on screen have a kind of fundamental digital equivalency. The notification of a new Friend Request has the same weight and excitement as the breaking news of a terrorist attack. Now, I know cognitively that one is more consequential than the other, but given that one is personal and immediate, while the other is impersonal and distant, it's actually a toss-up which I'm likely to choose. When this process occurs several dozen times per day, for years at a time, and for tens of millions of people, the potential effect on the self and society cannot be overstated. We are experiencing a transformation in the perception of reality.

The consensus from preliminary social research about this transformation is not promising for those concerned about democracy, social order, and truth. Though some researchers have noticed an increase in certain forms of social activism due to Internet use, such as the role of Twitter and Facebook in organizing during the Arab Spring protests, and the use of hashtags to raise awareness of faddish activist campaigns (#blacklivesmatter, #kony, etc.), the overwhelming effect appears to be a retreat from civic life and an increased apathy or lack of knowledge about social events.[48] The problem arises from the same traits that make digital life wonderful and world-changing. It is an instantaneous tsunami of unrelated content that changes every few seconds. iCulture is thrilling, like watching a live broadcast of everyone's life, as it is being lived. The wave of content is actually far too much to consume, however. Most users navigate this barrage using a variety of intermediaries that largely reduce and organize the flow according to their specifications. As suggested above, the dominant technique of organization is similarity. YouTube, iTunes, Amazon, and even The New York Times sends more of what it thinks you like based on past patterns. Fox News, MSNBC, and CNN have been using the same tactic for years. It is safe, evidence-based marketing approach. It is also the institutionalization of confirmation bias.

Confirmation bias is one of the most powerful and validated phenomena in social psychology. In plain terms: we choose the facts that fit with our existing beliefs. Confirmation bias screens out unfamiliar or challenging ideas or preferences. The psychological objective is safety and comfort. To the mind, ideas that are divergent or new are threatening, most likely because they require significant mental effort (brains are cognitive misers, psychologists tell us), and often, they are also emotionally upsetting. Most of us have spent the better part of our lives building our worldviews. Our sense of self is intricately bound up in them. Strange and contrary information is jarring to the self. And that's just one more stressor I don't need.

Truth is also incompatible with confirmation bias, by definition. The veracity of a claim has nothing to do with my opinion of it, logically speaking. For example, social science tells me that the death penalty has no effect on crime deterrence, and is more expensive than incarceration or rehabilitation. I dislike this finding and feel emotionally that it should not be so. How should I respond? If I am bestowed with a unusual dose of reasonableness and Old Culture, I might allow that the statement is true, and align my opinions with the truth. This is rare indeed, but it is actually the entire objective of science and education, the movement from ignorance to knowledge. However, I might also acknowledge the facticity of the statement, but persist in my position out of value-rational commitments. After all, as a U.S. congressmen famously said, "Don't confuse me with the facts; my mind is made up." But confirmation bias predicts a different and more disturbing outcome: I will avoid this information altogether and instead proactively seek out information that supports my view. I may only subscribe to news outlets that I agree with, only interact with those who share my view, and otherwise mentally segregate myself from opposing perspectives. Truth in this context is what I define it to be, which is to say, not truth in any meaningful sense. It is truthiness.

The triumph of truthiness over truth is aided by a bottomless ocean of "information providers" in iCulture, unprecedented in diversity and accessibility in human history. The issue, however, is quality control. In the days of Old Culture, we audiences entrusted professional curators of information known as "journalists" to provide us with only the news and perspective that met high standards of fact-checking, multiple sourcing, and objectivity, among others. Moreover, these curators were the primary providers of information, thus doubly ensuring that our informational diet was high quality. Finally, the news arrived at most twice per day, once with the morning newspaper and perhaps once again around dinner time via television. It was believed that it took at least that long to properly prepare a news story for public consumption.

None of this is true today. Americans are as likely to get their news from The Daily Show, Rush Limbaugh, or their Facebook feed as from Bob Schieffer of CBS News. But these sources are still a magnitude of quality greater than the constantly expanding population of questionable outlets available in the "blogosphere" or through user-edited sources such as Wikipedia or YouTube. If I am interested in finding "studies," "sources," or "articles" to support my claim that the death penalty is effective, there will be no shortage. Truth in iCulture is completely optional.

The implications of iCulture for democracy and ethics are profound yet hard to initially recognize. First, it has the potential to transform citizens into mere consumers. People may gradually lose the capacity to see themselves as more than audiences and buyers, both passive roles, rather than equal stakeholders in the outcome of their communities. Social observers such as Nicholas Carr and Sherry Turkle have already noted the mechanisms behind and initial signs of this transformation, and what they portend for the future of politics and social order. Second, iCulture's emphasis on the sensation of *feeling* good eclipses a concern on *being* good or *creating* good. The passivity and hedonism subtly cultivated through iCulture cannot simultaneously value altruism, proactive generosity, and social responsibility. The "i" in iCulture is not accidental; the ego-self is the universal audience of 21st century media and technology, and it is committed to the pleasure of "I" even if it produces enormous negligence or harm to many unseen others.

It is for precisely this reason that sociology is needed. It is also exactly why spiritual practice is urgently necessary. And I as have argued, these are merely two ways of doing the same thing.

What is that thing? At their core, sociology and spiritual practice are dedicated to *truth seeking*. Sociology, after all is the socially applied version of the natural science method that is dedicated to discovering what is real and how it works. The cradle of science was not curiosity, as we are sometimes led to believe in sanitized history books, but a persistent frustration with religious authority merely dictating the nature of the world. What became science began as a raw mixture of rebellion and doubt, with a good measure of intelligence and courage dashed in. Early scientists were possessed with a passion to discover, using reason and good evidence, the truth about the Earth, its origin, its inhabitants, and how the entire mechanism operates, independent of the stories they had been told about it. Social scientists likewise seek to know and tell others the truth about human beings, their tendencies, patterns, and history. Truth-telling, despite its current unpopularity, is the sociological reason for being.

With similar motive but very different technique, spiritual practice is equally committed to truth. Spiritual practice, however, typically involves the path of interior knowing, usually through contemplation, meditation, or experience. As the inspiring Hermann Hesse wrote, "I have been and still am a seeker, but I have ceased to question stars and books; I have begun to listen to the teaching my blood whispers to me."[49] The truth sought by spiritual practitioners is that inner truth of the heart, akin to intuition, which transcends evidence and contains also an element of decency and peace. This is, for all relevant purposes of truth, that greater reality which somehow is beyond history and particularities yet shines through them with force in critical moments. As in science, there is a real sense of courage in this spiritual seeking of Truth. It is for this reason that Gandhi called his lifelong nonviolent struggle for freedom and justice "experiments in Truth."

Sociology at its best is a spiritual practice than can deepen our commitment to truth seeking and truth telling. It can inure us to the temptations of iCulture and its many variations and instead show us a path to more meaningful, enduring, and helpful way of being that is, in the spirit of Alan Watts, "sincere without being serious." Sociology at its best is not only a human science, but a humane science. It explains without explaining away, and lifts people up rather than just being "uplifting." Any spiritual practice without a commitment to truth can easily degenerate into Pollyannaish denial or empty escapism. An insistence on truth (and Truth) can keep sociology vulnerable and human, as well as keeping spiritual practices grounded and clear-eyed.

Beyond this common foundation in truth, a few other important traits reveal the fundamental shared mission of sociology and spiritual practice. These include the experience of revelation, the pursuit of knowledge and its application, and the reliance on community. While the language of each may appear superficially different, it becomes clear that they are indeed conveying the same message.

Revelation

The history of science is replete with stories of discoveries that have come not through persistence, tedious hours in the lab, or intense cogitation of a problem. Instead, the solution arrived through an immediate breakthrough or spontaneous resolution—a "eureka" moment. These nonrational events often occur after long periods of deliberate and focused effort, but hardly ever occur as a forced result of that process. Typically, the mind, weary from rational exertion, is forced to surrender to or abandon the project for a time. After a time, often weeks or months, the solution appears clear as day in a sudden, ecstatic moment of total clarity. Those lucky enough to have such experiences frequently describe it as "the greatest moment of my life," "the happiest sensation possible," and even in quasi-religious terms, such "epiphany" or "revelation."

A famous example of this experience is provided by the greatest of modern scientists, Albert Einstein. Einstein was actually the beneficiary of many scientific epiphanies, though this first one helped produce his most significant contribution. One night, after working for several months to resolve the tensions between the view of physics held by Maxwell and Newton, he remembered riding in an automobile in Switzerland. He recalled looking back at the clock tower residing at top of the city's center courthouse. He imagined the streetcar dashing away from the clock tower at the speed of light. What would that feel like from both within the car and within the tower? He knew that from within the speeding car, the time on the clock tower would appear at a near dead stop. But if he were to look at his own watch within the car, it would appear to tick along normally. Eureka! Einstein concluded that time is relative, keeping a different pace depending on how fast we move, with faster objects experiencing a slower rate of time. "A storm broke loose in my mind," he wrote, and the theory of relativity was created. Later, Einstein would write of his many nonrational encounters with truth, "Everyone who is seriously involved in the pursuit of science becomes convinced that a spirit is manifest in the laws of the Universe-a spirit vastly superior to that of man, and one in the face of which we with our modest powers must feel humble."[50]

Most working sociologists (and even a number of sociology students) have their own personal stories of such "aha!" moments. Weber's landmark *The Protestant Ethic and the Spirit of Capitalism* would likely have never been written had he not spent three months in the United States during the midpoint of that work in 1904. Weber, recovering from a devastating depression, found immediate inspiration and validation for his provocative thesis linking religion and economic dynamics through the vibrant evangelical Protestantism of North Carolina, where he lingered for several weeks before moving on to that capitol of capitalism, New York City.

In my own research life, the experience of revelation has been infrequent but miraculously well-timed. After two years collecting and analyzing data on nearly 500 Christian activist groups for my dissertation, I despaired at the lack of significant or interesting results. I had confirmed a few unremarkable findings from other researchers and created a handful of lackluster descriptive results. Weeks of combing through the data, scouring the tables, and running endless analyses produced nothing. I was ready to give up. As an escape from the undertow of Soc Sadness, I began to grade essays for the social theory class for which I was a teaching assistant. One student paper was about Talcott Parson's theory of social equilibrium as applied to American politics. The paper was dreadfully written and poorly argued, but sparked a bit of an epiphany for me: What if civil society was governed by the principle of balance? Was there evidence in the Christian activist sector for the social equilibrium that Pareto, Parsons, Shils, and many others had seen in their analyses? I had been fixated on the outcomes of these social movement organizations and had not considered the cultural ecosystem in which they all inhabited. I spent an afternoon analyzing the proportion of progressive and conservative groups per decade between 1960 and 2000.

The result was revelatory: in each time period, the number of progressive and conservative Christian organizations was almost exactly equal. Somehow, a type of homeostasis of the civil sphere was occurring. I was not looking for this outcome, nor was I even equipped to see it. But with a new frame, a different perspective, I was finally able to find the gem amidst all the rocks. Unlike the revelations of Einstein and Weber, my little gem has not changed the world. But at least I know what it feels like, and that a force beyond my conscious mind was behind it.

These experiences of spontaneous insights into tough problems and new-found energy occur at unexpected times and in moments of clear tranquility, often after having almost given up on the problem. It appears the mind requires a period of incubation for the subconscious powers to render an indirect but perfect solution. This period of quiet, internal reorganization and creative stewing has a name familiar to those with a background in spiritual practice: meditation.

It is no accident that the most influential writing of Descartes, one of the founders of modern science, was titled *Meditations*. Descartes' method of radical self-emptying and focused introspection bears a striking resemblance to the process engaged by mystical Christians, Jews, Buddhists, and similar contemplative practitioners for millennia. It is, in fact, identical to the method used by Siddhartha Gautauma on his way to enlightenment and Buddhahood. Spiritual traditions the world over emphasize, to a shockingly similar degree, the importance of quiet waiting for answers. In the Quaker tradition, the entire primary service is waiting for the Light to join them and inspire devotees to share their experience with others. In Islam, the holy season of Ramadan is spent in prayerful fasting and purification. Devoted Muslims wait from dawn to sunset to eat, and abstain from most worldly activities during the holy month. Zen

Buddhists sit in zazen for many hours each day, days on end, waiting for the moment of *satori*, which is said to be a sudden realization of truth and knowledge. Described in William James' classic *The Varieties of Religious Experience*, satori and the eureka moment are virtually indistinguishable.

If it can be said that humanity's spiritual traditions were the first to discover the experience of revelatory truth, it cannot be said that they have a monopoly on it. As we have clearly observed from science and philosophy, revelation belongs to humanity, a part of its species birthright. However, it is likely the case that in modern life, the two most common routes to revelation are spiritual practice and scientific inquiry. I suspect that most scientists and many sociologists enter their vocation in pursuit of more of these types of peak experiences. The moment of revelation is one of the purest feelings of bliss and satisfaction that a human being can know, whether found in the pursuit of answers for the external world or that of the internal realm. As a discipline that seeks to in a sense harmonize these worlds, sociology is one of the most fruitful revelatory practices that we can follow.

Knowledge

In the introduction to Earl Babbie's widely used *The Practice of Social Research*, the author asks, "What is the purpose of social research?" The answers are straightforward and accurate: *exploration, description, and explanation*. As true as these may be, they do not actually address the core question. What, after all, is the purpose of exploration, description, and explanation? These are left as either uninteresting or unnecessary queries. This is true for most branches of science. Knowledge—the purported result of exploration, description, and explanation—is seen as an end in itself when it is even examined.

Why in particular do sociologists want to know things? In addition to those reasons offered by Babbie, it appears sociologists seek knowledge for one slightly less rational motive: to improve the lives of human beings. Unlike insights from psychology and economics, sociology has rarely (to my knowledge) been used deliberately to control, manipulate, or exploit humanity. In fact, many sociological findings have been put to practice for the explicit purpose of liberation and humane advancement. My own subfield of social movement research is well-known for its application in the area of political activism and strategic democracy. The work of nonviolent strategist Gene Sharp and political sociologist Charles Tilly are but two exemplars put to good purpose in the Philippines, Arab Spring, and Occupy movements.

But, as any good physician will tell you, in order to be able to fix a problem, we must understand it. We must understand its components, processes, history, and tendencies. We must first take time to make observations, collect evidence, and correct previous understandings. We have to put aside prior information or received "wisdom" on the subject and investigate the phenomenon as they we had never seen it before. In my Introductory courses, I assign students a writing task of assuming the role of an anthropologist from another planet, the "alien journalist" point of view. If you had never seen Earth or human beings before, what would you notice about them? What are their salient traits and habits? This practice helps cultivate the perspective of the "sociological imagination" described by C. Wright Mills. The sociological imagination, it turns out, is functionally equivalent to one of the oldest and most revered ideas in Eastern spirituality, "beginner's mind." A term popularized by Zen teacher D.T. Suzuki, beginner's mind is the adult form of *tabula rasa*, the blank slate of empty, pure awareness known mostly to human infants. Beginner's mind takes nothing for granted. Nothing is seen as better or worse than anything else. Judgments are bracketed and held as inadmissible. Simple observation and description is the only practice. Careful attention to minute detail is encouraged. As Zen poet Gary Snyder wrote of walking meditation, "The foot is aware not only of every groove of the floor, but also of the foot itself."[51] I describe this state of consciousness as "Sherlock Mode." The celebrated detective brilliantly brought to life by Benedict Cumberbatch is a nondiscriminating observation radar dish, picking up every possible speck of data and comparing it to the database of past samples. The analysis can then begin.

That oldest and most elementary form of sociological data collection, the census, does not really begin to be interesting until we add in a comparative perspective. In 2010, census-takers counted 308 million Americans. Big deal. What's interesting is what they say in the next sentence: "a 9.7 % increase compared to the 2000 Census." Data is only empty symbols without context and an interpretation. Knowing this provokes a series of further questions: Where is most of the growth? Among what types of Americans? What does this mean for schools, economies, and our national culture? And on and on. Knowledge is always value-neutral. How we as social scientists use this highly detailed information about our society depends on our goals, which ultimately depend on our moral codes.

Sociologists, however, are also interested in how humans create those very moral codes! And their effects, their differences, and their change over time. In fact, much of my own research is on this very question. Sociologists are among the few researchers who recognize that knowledge and truth are themselves irreducibly social products, always and everywhere made by humans in social contexts. Therefore, there is a large and productive subfield of our discipline known as the sociology of knowledge. Peter Berger, my former colleague and one of the leading figures in the sociology of religion, began as a sociologist of knowledge, for example.[52] What does it mean or matter that knowledge is a social product? For one, it means that knowledge will always bear the mark of the social structure, culture, and historical moment in which it is found. That is, knowledge is not entirely timeless, despite what the great overpowering chorus of the masses will sometimes assert. For another, knowledge is not inevitable or universally available. It is, for example, highly improbable that a culture such as the Roman Empire could have developed the idea of universal suffrage. Likewise, it is very difficult for today's 15 year-olds to conclude that the Iraq War was a necessary and just exercise, but the opposite was true only a decade ago. Knowledge is as much an artifact of the times as a fragment of earthen pottery or arrowhead.

Finally, how any particular knowledge is put to use (if at all) is also profoundly determined by the social system in which it emerges. A clear example is provided by the very different use of the state to address human needs in the United States versus the European Union versus China. All three now have at least a half-century of knowledge produced by social science and historical experience to enable them to generate revenue, distribute resources, and manage externalities such as pollution. Yet each culture, because of the tremendous differences in values, norms, and goals, have developed radically divergent systems for managing these demands. In the U.S., the state is used to a moderate degree to regulate both markets and pollution. In the E.U, the state is brought more heavily to bear on both, with a reduction in private profits and freedom deemed acceptable by its citizens. In China, the state is deeply involved in economic production and distribution, but has taken hardly any steps toward environmental regulation. More knowledge would not necessarily be of assistance. The sociocultural landscape of each determines not only how knowledge is used, but what even counts as legitimate knowledge.[53]

Gifts of Truth

When applied, the knowledge gained through sociological techniques and thinking can be enormously useful. Apart from the vocational ends thousands of undergraduates apply it toward every year, sociological knowledge is helpful for everyday purposes that go beyond the office. One of these is *standing up for truth*. Many students report back to me that their exposure to sociology has helped them in dinner conversations or family reunions when truth is under attack. This can take many forms. One common form unfortunately is what I call the Gravy Boat Racist. Invariably around Thanksgiving, Christmas, or other major holiday, a member of the family will say something offensive or erroneous about another race group while food is being passed around the table. A version heard recently by my students involved why African-Americans "always burn down their neighborhood" and "destroy businesses of hard-working people" after a black person is beaten or killed by police. The most heard explanation is that "that's just the way they are," or "they are inherently more violent than whites."

A more perfect Sociological Teaching Moment could not be produced. Armed with heads full of research data, sociology students can quickly dissect the fallacies of this argument and challenge the speaker with insight about the true nature of these incidents. Double-standards of media coverage for white and black protestors, the overwhelming size of peaceful protests compared to violent looting, the long history of police brutality in these neighborhoods, and the fundamental role of poverty and low opportunities are among just a few of the suitable evidence-based retorts. Simply responding in this way tends to paralyze the Gravy Boat Racist, and if not, they are at least encouraged to provide similar facts to support their claims. It often stops right there. This exchange is not always easy or pleasant for the young sociologist, who may be accused of being elitist or an egghead, or simply given the silent treatment. Standing up for truth is never easy. But one does not have to be Rosa Parks for Cesar Chavez either. One just needs a little bit of knowledge and the courage to talk back to the Gravy Boat Racist who has probably never been challenged before.

Standing up for truth does not have to be even this confrontational. Upon returning to visit after graduation, sociology alumni frequently confess they find themselves starting more and more sentences with, "Um, actually…" They are The Correctors; those who refuse to let half-truths, myths, and outright deception go unchecked. Admittedly, these people are often annoying. But better, I tell them, to be a little annoying then to let a known lie get passed around as the truth and do a lot of damage. In this way, sociological knowledge acts as a countermeasure to deceit, much of which is practiced in service of manipulation and power grabs. Politics is the arena of life in which we see this the most. I would even venture that if there were more sociologists or sociologically armed citizens, many politicians would not hold their current offices. The lies, distortions, and myths they used to hoodwink voters would have been nullified on contact with the minds of these data-powered listeners. Knowledge of any kind is useful in this way, but sociological knowledge is uniquely powerful because many of the false claims made by unscrupulous politicians have to do with social, cultural, and historical processes. In a way, a person versed in the social sciences is the worst nightmare of an aspiring politician. This explains, actually, why federal funding for social science research is always threatened and at the top of every year's budget chopping block.

Closely related to the spiritual necessity of standing up for truth is the cultivation of courage. Sociological knowledge *makes us braver*. One of the major reasons people do not take a stand against an intellectual bully or grocery line bigot is that they feel they lack the facts and expertise to make a good argument. Personally, I have heard this dozens of times dating back to when I was a high school debater. Debate, like sociology, prepares one for rhetorical combat. Like boot camp, it confronts the novice with so many battle simulations and so much training that when real war happens, fear is absent and only rationality and practice take over. If taught well and deeply ingrained, sociological knowledge and training can give us the evidence and perspective we need in everyday arguments to represent our side well. More importantly, having more intellectual ammunition strengthens our confidence and gives us the resolve needed to engage adversaries in the first place.

Finally, and perhaps obviously, sociological knowledge makes us *better thinkers.* This is not necessarily true of every academic discipline. The best description I've ever heard about this came from a graduating senior who was double majoring in sociology and accounting. She said, "Accounting classes just filled my mind with information. It was like high school. Sociology taught me how to *use my mind* for the first time." This is the original essence of education. How exactly was she taught to use her mind? First, sociology drills in the subtle art of observation, the foundation of all science. The type of observation taught by sociology is a bit different, though. It emphasizes seeing familiar things through a new lens, making the old and taken for granted new and almost foreign. Like Zen, sociology uses the same mind but in totally novel ways. As the proverb by Hsin Hsin Ming says: "

> At first, I saw mountains as mountains and rivers as rivers. Then, I saw mountains were not mountains and rivers were not rivers. Finally, I see mountains again as mountains, and rivers again as rivers."[54]

Through the sociological lens, reality takes on a fresh, fascinating glint. We begin to see, rather than merely look.

But we don't stop with observation. We then make measurements, collect more data, draw comparisons, and form hypotheses. We try to figure out what's going and how it got this way. We use our minds in innovative and creative ways to form explanations, accounts, and predictions. Instead of being content with the information provided by others (memorization), we develop our own understandings and compare them with the ideas of others. This is the rationale for the literature review process. We try to improve upon the work of others and extend human knowledge in novel directions. Creation and originality are the markers of intellectual maturity, and precious little in modern education cultivates these capacities. Sociology at its best keeps our minds nimble, as we confront everyday social reality with new questions and challenge conventional ways of looking at the world. In the process, we become both more creative and more alive, as the day presents an infinite variety of miracles to both understand and appreciate.

Community

Sociological knowledge, like most spiritual insight, is a collective product. True, many empirical findings are discovered through individual research, analysis, and writing. But ultimately, almost all sociological studies are vetted by a community of similarly trained scholars. This is the reason for the peer review process which comprises the heart of intellectual integrity for the entire scientific enterprise. An individual scholar may know that her project was conducted with the highest level of rigor and in dialogue with the best and most current theory in the field. But the strength of her conscientiousness and care is not enough. Her research must be evaluated by a qualified group of fellow scientists who must come to a rough consensus that the work is worthy of publication. Much like a tribunal of Talmudic experts, the academic community is the final arbiter of merit for social science. This trust of community is also reminiscent of the divided branches of government built into the U.S. Constitution, as well as the very nature of democracy, though the reliance on specialized experts is obviously higher in science. Nevertheless, the core wisdom behind all of them is the same: individuals are not competent appraisers of their own work.

It is for this reason that we find similar processes within the world's ancient spiritual traditions. Though Christian monks spend many hours per day in solitude, whether in contemplation, prayer, or physical labor, they generally live within monastic communities. These others provide not only needed social and emotional support, but a check on their spiritual development and insights. Brothers are encouraged to discuss their mystical experiences, should they have any, with the abbot or other trusted monks in order to help them understand what they have learned and also for the community to prevent the individual from straying too far with his own interpretation or method. This is also the basis for the "Three Gems" of Buddhism, in which devotees pledge to take refuge in the Buddha (the model for awakening), the *dharma* (the teachings of the Buddha), and the *sangha* (the community of fellow Buddhists, akin to a congregation). Not only do communities such as these provide a check on individual truth-seeking adventures (necessary for any group that wishes to survive), but the community also actively assists in the interpretation, cultivation, and improvement of the individual's work, which it often needs.

The discipline of sociology then, could be seen as a large *sangha* or monastic community. Sociology, like any spiritual practice, needs a supportive social and intellectual structure in which to properly develop. Whether a student taking an Introductory course or a tenured professor seeking his 50th peer-reviewed article, sociologists can provide a friendly, welcoming, and constructive environment to one another with the goal of producing better ideas to create a better world. When it works well, this is precisely what good university departments, graduate schools, and reviewers do. Too often, though, practitioners lose sight of the spiritual and constructive aspect of their work and ego-based motives dominate. Should we find ourselves participating in the sociological *sangha*, we should endeavor to make it a place of true refuge, a community of mutual support and growth.

Chapter Five

Virtue

"Happiness is the meaning and the purpose of life,
the whole aim and end of human existence."

—*Aristotle*

"Those who are happiest are those who do the most for others."
—*Booker T. Washington,* Up from Slavery

"Maybe part of our formal education should be training in empathy.
Imagine how different the world would be if, in fact, that were
'reading, writing, arithmetic, empathy.'"

—*Neil deGrasse Tyson*

In 1993, former Secretary of Education William Bennett surprised the worlds of publishing and academia with the phenomenal success of his *The Book of Virtues*. Bennett's homespun brand of old-fashioned values struck an unexpected chord with an American reading audience dealing with Stage 5 Clinton fatigue. The backlash against relativism, moral decay, and political correctness had begun. Bennett's book ended up selling more than 2 million copies and was adapted for children and television.

That was as good as it got for virtue in popular culture.

Speaking of virtue in the 21st century is akin to discussing blacksmithing or shag carpet. You can do it, but few really take you seriously. In fact, when talking about this chapter with friends, I often encountered this dumbfounded countenance that seemed to indicate something like quaint amusement. They would frequently go on to say things that conveyed the anachronistic yet adorable nature of the subject:

"Virtue? Ohhkaaay... but what does that have to do with sociology?"
"Virtue? Like morals? You're not going to get preachy are you?"

This is not to say that these folks are opposed to virtue. But in the 21st century, it has become unfashionable and even rude to talk about it. Virtue talk implies a set of traits and actions that are better than others. Some argue that such talk sets up a relationship where one person has the right to evaluate another person, which creates hierarchy. Moreover, the person judging has no intrinsic authority to evaluate the other person, therefore their assessment is totally without merit. This reaction has created innumerable challenges for my other research area, the sociology of morality. The reaction can best be illustrated through the now-unforgettable statement made during one of my graduate seminars after I had presented some of my initial dissertation research. "I'm not sure if morality exists," said the tenured professor, "but if it does, you've done a good job describing how it works." It took every last ounce of restraint to stop me from replying, "Thanks. But what do you mean by 'good'?"

My treatment of virtue here need not carry the baggage of judgment, guilt, or inferiority. By virtue, I simply mean what the Random House English Dictionary means by the term:

virtue: (noun) a good or admirable quality or property[55]

Admittedly, a true ethical skeptic will balk at the usage of "good" in the definition, and demand that I provide compelling justification for asserting why a given virtue is good. My answer is not complicated; it is essentially Aristotle's:

good things are those which enhance the flourishing of the person and those they affect. In what follows, I will do my best to make a case for virtue, how it promotes flourishing, and how sociology is among the very best practices for cultivating it.

It is odd —at least today—to lean on ancient Greek philosophy within a book on sociology and spirituality. This is a shame. No one made a stronger case for virtue than Aristotle. After an extended period of intellectual exile, the late 20th century saw an unexpected revival of sorts for Aristotelian moral philosophy through what came to be down as "virtue ethics." Prominent names in this camp include G.E.M. Anscombe, Alasdair Macintyre, Rosalind Hursthouse, and Paul Ricouer. What follows is derived mostly from Aristotle alone, but is also represented within the main currents of virtue ethics without serious divergence.

Almost every dimension of Aristotle's ethics reflected a foundation in what he called "excellence in being human." This simple phrase is freighted with hidden meaning. He could have just as easily said, "being an excellent human." But that would be to distort one of the key and overlooked aspects of his ethics. Aristotle makes clear that virtue is not an inborn temperament or a single display of goodness. Virtue is the product of deliberate, directed effort. But it is *also a motive* of that effort. Thus virtue becomes Virtue, or virtuous intention is molded into virtuous character. He continues, "Men acquire a particular quality by constantly acting a particular way ... you become just by performing just actions, temperate by performing temperate actions, brave by performing brave actions."[56] Aristotle is building a case that an individual is largely a collection of their actions; you are what you have done and habitually do.

This is both a source of relief and distress. On the relief hand, it does not require that I "be good" or have "good thoughts" or a "noble heart." The mental state or attitude of the person is not central. Thus, any normal person with a chaotic cauldron of thoughts, some loving and kind, others perverse and simply infantile, can still behave admirably and thereby cultivate virtue. Whew. On the other hand...what most of us do habitually is nothing to be proud of. Screaming at idiot drivers, forgetting Dad's birthday 14 years in a row, and eating Krispy Kremes like we had a donut shaped hole in our soul is not going to build virtue. If virtue is a product of habit, the only way most of us can be virtuous is by transforming gluttony, sloth, and torpor into virtues.

But virtue ethicists provide hope. Even though handicapped by being philosophers, they retain an understanding of human nature rivaling that of normal people and sociologists. They recognize that it is indeed virtuous to *even make an attempt* at doing good, especially when it means overcoming one's natural impulses or suppressing natural drives. Therefore, great virtuous intent eventually brings about modest levels of virtue, even if mistakes and setbacks are made along the way. Indeed, some virtue ethicists even regard this "continence" as a purer form of virtue than the person endowed from birth with noble motives and no inner conflict, as it indicates a degree of perseverance, itself a potent variety of virtue.

Likewise, Aristotle stressed that virtue is a deeply internalized, durable tendency of a person, an orientation to the self and the world that manifests in distinct ways regardless of situation. Hursthouse refers to it as an "entrenched, multi-track disposition."[57] Thus, one-off instances of goodness or acting morally in a single dimension of life do not qualify as virtue.

For example, everyone agrees that Harry is the world's greatest family man. He attends every child's birthday party, always brings the perfect present, gives his wife a massage every evening after work, and writes poems for each family member at Christmas. He makes Atticus Finch look like a deadbeat. But what folks don't know is that Harry's construction business is profitable because he uses undocumented immigrant labor, whom he often doesn't pay. When he does pay, it is about half the minimum wage. A typical work day at Harry's site lasts 12 hours, and they work on Saturday. He provides one portable toilet and one jug of drinking water at the site. Last month, three workers were taken to the emergency room, two for heat stroke and one for dehydration. Harry, therefore, does not meet the Aristotelian criteria for virtue, though most of his neighbors would be surprised to learn this. If he had true virtue, his disposition toward goodness would be rather equally dispersed across his whole personality, rather than piled up in one area (family).

The bigger question, especially for those interested in sociology, not philosophy, is "Who cares?" Why is virtue important? Indeed, for many of us, something like, "I'm a good enough person. Isn't virtue a little archaic and irrelevant in the crazy modern world?" Great point. I tend to agree. Personally, my patience for virtue and the like would be very small indeed if not for one central wrinkle that relates to something I do care about: happiness.

For Aristotle, virtue was not a moralistic term, but almost a functional one. The objective of life was to be happy—*eudaimon*—and the most direct route was through virtue. Aristotle contrasted eudaimon, which is best translated as "well-being" or "flourishing," with pleasure seeking, what we would today call hedonism. He was the first to make a reasoned case that the former was not only superior, but what every human was deeply (though often unknowingly) searching for. Even in ancient Greece, well before iCulture and mass literacy, he noticed that most people settled for pleasure, which is inherently fleeting and unpredictable (though intense), rather than put in the work that led to well-being. He wrote,

> "Well-being does not consist in amusement. In fact, it would be strange if our end were amusement, and if we were to labor and suffer hardships all our life long merely to amuse ourselves...Flourishing is regarded as a life in conformity with virtue. It is a life which involves effort and is not spent in amusement...."[58]

With this formulation, virtue ethicists advance a provocative and helpful premise: human well-being is an objective condition. As opposed to pleasure, external observers can ascertain whether another person or group is flourishing, or rank their relative well-being. As Hursthouse rightly notes, only the individual can say if they are happy, and they are the only authority that counts.[59] Such an innovation is of potentially great aid in sociology, but also in life generally.

It helps us explain, for example, how a person with millions in the bank and servants to clean the palace can still, if you ask them, say they are miserable. Or why, as recent studies report, some of the happiest people on earth have no running water or reliable food supplies. Thus well-being (an objective state) and happiness (a subjective state) are disentangled. In most cases, however, they are in alignment. It is difficult, for example, to have your home searched each day by a foreign army and keep a smile on your face. Objective and subjective status are therefore separate markers but closely correlated.

In modern parlance, eudaimonia might be roughly understood by the phrase "health and wellness," provided it is understood to include all the dimensions of human experience. These include optimal emotional, physical, social/relational, sexual, economic, and intellectual well-being. In other words, the best bestness across the best things. Peachy. Who wouldn't want that? But here, where it could get woefully boring and flimsy, is where Aristotle drops the punch line:

My well-being depends on your well-being.

Hmm...it seems like...I've heard that...somewhere before...

This is Aristotle's version of *ubuntu* from Chapter 3. Just as ubuntu is a statement about the interdependence between the self and others, eudaimonia puts that recognition in a normative context by stating that *our flourishing is interdependent as well*. Virtue ethics, though predating formal sociology by a couple of millennia, profoundly reflects the truths uncovered by the social sciences. The chief example is seeing others (society) as what Aristotle called "a second self." This tenet states that any "other" person should be seen as an extension of myself; that any apparent division between oneself and other humans is not ultimately real. This view is supported by evidence from modern sociology, and has tremendous implications for ethics. First, as suggested above, it means that for me to truly thrive, you must also thrive. For you to suffer while I flourish is not really possible because I participate in your humanity and vice versa. Thus your diminishment is mine. Second, it implies that the greatest well-being will occur when both of us flourish roughly at the same level. Therefore, there is a strong argument for egalitarianism built into the system. Finally, I can relax a little about my own surviving and thriving because I know that you are invested in my well-being by virtue (pun intended) of the same principle. Interestingly, a motive such as "self-interest" is rendered near meaningless by this understanding of eudaimonia. Solely pursuing my own interest will actually backfire and cause me suffering if it does not also increase the well-being of others to a near equal degree.

The part of me that is a sociologist of religion is elated to learn this, as it is almost identical with the ethical teachings of the world's great spiritual traditions. Here's just one example, taken from a recent interview with the 14th Dalai Lama, Tenzin Gyatso:

> "All he [His Holiness] is really saying is that we are all a part of a single body, and to think of 'I' and 'you,' of the right hand's interests being different from the left's, makes no sense at all. It's crazy to impede your neighbor, because he is as intrinsic to your welfare as your thumb is. It's almost absurd to say you wish to get ahead of your colleague—it's like your right toe saying it longs to be ahead of the left."[60]

Virtue is also central to living well in Taoism, still a major religion in much of the Far East. In Taoism, the "way"—*tao*—is the natural course of nature. The person who is in sync with tao is said to possess *te*, a kind of inner strength or potency that arises from their trust in the tao. Te is most often translated into English as "virtue," as its lived quality has a strong moral aspect, akin to integrity.

Christianity, of course, has from its earliest forms preached the cultivation of virtue, broken down into the theological and cardinal virtues. Theological virtues, as articulated in 1 Corinthians 13:13, are faith, hope, and love. To these are added the so-called cardinal virtues of prudence, justice, temperance, and courage, borrowed from Aristotle and Greek philosophy as a whole. Christian moral philosophy and virtue ethics share many common features. Alasdair

Macintyre, author of the influential *After Virtue* and a central figure in contemporary virtue ethics, is Roman Catholic, while Stanley Hauerwas, author of *Vision and Virtue*, is Methodist.

Beyond the realm of religion, the core tenets of virtue ethics have been picked up by major movements in the human sciences. In psychology, Martin Seligman and Christopher Peterson's research into "positive psychology," is premised on discovering the cultivation of those qualities that produce optimal psychological well-being, analogous to eudaimonia. Their work identified six categories of "Character Strengths and Virtues" that had "a surprising amount of similarity across cultures and strongly indicated a historical and cross-cultural convergence."[61] These six categories of virtue are courage, justice, humanity, temperance, transcendence, and wisdom. Seligman and Peterson note that behavioral interventions designed to assist the client in the development or enhancement of these virtues resulted in improvements in emotional health and stability.

Virtue, then, is not simply about an individual's character. It has a necessary social dimension. Its objective is the greatest, sustainable well-being for all persons. The vehicle by which this flourishing is achieved is the cultivation of a number of deeply ingrained traits that work together to form a coherent moral disposition seen across the whole of a person's life. As a result, virtue has obvious sociological effects. But is the reverse true? Can sociology cultivate virtue itself? For many practicing sociologists, I suspect the answer would be "Not really," or "That's an irrelevant question." Certainly, it is not the expressed function or purpose of sociology. But in our field we have a term—latent function—that I think best describes the relationship of sociology to virtue. A latent function occurs inadvertently or in addition to the primary or "manifest function" of the mechanism. Sometimes the latent function is never fully recognized by those involved, but it occurs, often to great effect, all the same.

Little academic research exists on the effects of sociology on a person's ethical life or well-being. It would be welcome. However, it's not clear that such systematic studies would reveal more insights than direct observation over more than decade of cases. And it would certainly not reveal more sincere and deeply

felt insights than those that I've personally experienced over that period. Therefore, what follows is a case for the virtue-building power of sociology based
mostly on my own life in teaching and studying sociology. Put simply, I know
sociology can make us better people because it worked on me. Despite my best
effort to remain "normal" and Comfortably Numb (thanks Pink Floyd), it got
me. And I've never been so glad to be wrong.

Mindfulness: The First Gift

C. Wright Mills is best known for three things: (1) riding motorcycles at dan-
gerously high speeds en route to eat a massive steak dinner that would kill a
mere mortal; (2) writing a great book on elites in America; and (3) introducing
us to the idea of the "sociological imagination." The sociological imagination is
one of the first terms that Introduction to Sociology students hear. I say "hear"
because it is actually rare for an introductory student to actually understand
the term, even after months of explanation or regular usage. I had this difficulty myself as a freshman in college, and my freshmen today often have the
same trouble. The problem with the term is that it presumes the student knows
what "sociological" means in the first place. This would be akin to a philosophy
instructor asking her novice students to be "epistemically cognizant" as they
read the material for class. Many introductory students hear the word "sociology" for the first time in college. Most have a vague but often inaccurate notion
about the meaning (usually something more like social psychology). Moreover,
the term "imagination" leaves many students with a rather fanciful impression
of the field. Imagination is a purely creative, nonjudgmental, free-form exercise.
We are accustomed to telling young children to "use their imagination" when
playing outdoors. So they imagine they are pirates, superheroes, doctors, were-
wolves, and so on. And they can't be wrong.

But that's not what is meant by the term "imagination" in Mills' sense.
Because of this confusion, I opt instead, during the first half of the semester, for
"paying deep attention" or "social mindfulness." This is grasped much more easily.
"Paying attention" in the conventional way is already understood, which makes
"deep attention" intriguing yet relatable. But mindfulness is normally a spiritual

term, so its application to social science also piques their interest. More importantly, mindfulness is a virtue, indeed the doorway to all the others, in my view. As such it is the First Gift of Sociology and the starting point for all spiritual practices.

The reason that mindfulness is an appropriate substitute for the sociological imagination is that the results are effectively the same. For example, a classic exercise for using the sociological imagination is to look at the tags in one's clothing. The countries where the garments are made are then put on the board. The patterns that emerge are striking. Almost no developed countries (U.S., U.K., Australia, etc.) are mentioned. Countries that make apparel today are almost entirely "periphery" countries—those with large surplus labor forces, low per capita income, and little domestic production of their own. Then working conditions, wages, and environmental policies in these countries are discussed. Asked to reflect mindfully on this situation, students regularly surface feelings of guilt, outrage, and complicity in the problem. In my classes, I also ask students to apply this way of thinking to any product or service they purchase, as the fundamental structures are similar. Buying a burger from a fast-food chain is not as thoughtless as it was before. Filling up the gas tank is now a minor moral dilemma.

Mindfulness in the traditional spiritual meaning always suggests being fully awake. Not merely alert and energized, but one's whole **mind fully** available and receptive. It means not being half asleep, in a kind of zombie state of conformity. It means not only acting and thinking but acting *while* thinking, a reflexive state of critical awareness. Critical in the sense of a deeper mode of consciousness, rather than negative or fault-finding. This mindfulness sees connections. It, for instance, knows that there is a direct relationship between the number of payday loan providers in my city and my lack of involvement with the city council to limit their numbers. Or the amount of plastic bags near the riverbank and my neighbor's opposition to a ban on such bags at grocery stores. And so on. Mindfulness, therefore, includes a dimension of conscientiousness and a brave degree of introspection. True mindfulness with a sociological lens added does not allow me to see myself as somehow separate from or not implicated in the social world around and its problems. In this way, it brings to life with contemporary vitality C. Wright Mills' notion of the link between "personal troubles and public issues."

With mindfulness established as a regular mode of consciousness, a new lens on the world, the other virtues are more easily contacted and cultivated. As with any aspect of a spiritual practice, they require daily attention and a discipline of devotion. With time, however, most practitioners find that the activity is self-perpetuating, as the rewards of virtue build eudaimonia and the fruits become visible in one's relational, moral, and emotional life.

Empathy

Without doubt, the greatest virtue fostered through sociology is empathy. Though our culture is fairly effective in encouraging *sympathy*—feeling for others, akin to pity—it is not skilled, in the main, in nurturing empathy— feeling with others. In fact, some scholars observe that contemporary American society is engendering the opposite, a kind of callous narcissism and a pace of life that makes empathy seem like an indulgent emotional luxury.[62]

Empathy is sometimes described as feeling what others feel, or "standing in their shoes." This is accurate but partial, as empathy includes both an emotional and cognitive component. The emotional experience is essentially recognizing and sharing the feeling state of another person, particular rendered through facial expression, vocalization, or body language. This capacity is present in infants and appears to be a natural capacity of normal human brains. Cognitive empathy, which is also sometimes referred to as "theory of mind" or perspective taking, is the ability to accurately imagine another's experience. Cognitive empathy is an advanced psychological experience, one that does not develop in humans until roughly the age of five. Levels of empathy, however, are highly variable in both children and adults, and various factors contribute to these differences. Genetics, neurodevelopmental factors (such as the formation of mirror neurons in the prefrontal cortex), temperament, quality of relationships, and regular engagement with prosocial activities are among the key players in the level and extent of empathic development.[63] When one or more of these fails, various disorders of empathy can result, such as autism, sociopathy, or psychopathy. As the beloved late film critic Roger Ebert said, "I believe empathy is the most essential quality of civilization."[64] Truly, without the capacity to feel, understand, and care about the condition of others, the prospects for forging human societies of any durability are dim. Instead Rousseau and Locke's "state of nature" prevails with only the "fit" surviving and only as long as they remain fit. Social cooperation, family life, and morality itself are only meaningful in the context of a highly developed and inclusive sense of empathy. It is a bit surprising, then, that sociology, the field most interested in the sociality of human beings, has taken only a passing and very recent interest in empathy.

The world's spiritual traditions, however, have more than made up for it. No human trait is of more central and universal interest to them than this "feeling and understanding of others." Norbert Elias, Sigmund Freud, and even Friedrich Nietzsche held that spirituality and religion are the key factor in the "civilizing process," brought about in large measure by the tendency of them to promote empathy. The most helpful form of empathy for civilizing is that directed toward nonkin and strangers, known as "out-group perspective-taking" in psychology. In-group empathy is almost automatic given normal socialization and child-development. But developing nearly the same level of concern, generosity, and kindness toward those unlike oneself has required, historically, unusual interventions at the level of teachings, directives, and stories. That is, through culture, not through instinct or evolutionary drives. Cultural forms such as religious commandments, parables, and precepts, reinforced with a degree of sacred or transcendent authority were among the first forces to deeply move human societies toward anything resembling civilization. The prototypical version of this empathic instruction is the "golden rule," found in various configurations in every major world religion, past and present: "That which you want for yourself, seek for mankind"[65] is the phrasing in Islam. Perhaps the strongest expression in the Christian tradition is Jesus' command in the fifth chapter of the Gospel of Matthew, "But I say, love your enemies and pray for those who persecute you."

But the world's spiritual traditions are not the only place where empathy may be nurtured. Indeed, in the modern world, fewer people are having regular contact with these lineages. Therefore, in my view, empathy is the greatest moral contribution of sociology, and perhaps its greatest contribution all told. Properly taught and seriously studied, sociology can be the most profound opportunity for empathic growth in a young modern's life. The sociology classroom is one of the few locations in contemporary life where a person still being shaped into maturity can encounter the experience of a stranger and be guided toward feeling, understanding, and acting toward their well-being. They can learn not only about the life conditions of the suffering millions, but also be moved to identify with these as similar to themselves or those they love. Sociology is uniquely equipped with both the empirical facts and the holistic perspective to tackle this critical task.

How exactly does sociology cultivate the virtue of empathy? First, we must understand what the potential barriers to empathy are that sociology is effective at removing. The most important is what I call the Myth of Deserve. Humans in general but Americans in particular are deeply attached to the narrative of deservingness, which is a version of meritocracy, the idea that success comes to those who most merit it, usually by way of their effort or sacrifice. Within a few weeks in a typical sociology classroom, the Myth of Deserve is on its way to the Island of Misfit Ideas. One graph courtesy of the Current Population Survey from the Census Bureau drives this point home with stunning clarity:

Americans Raised at the Top and Bottom Are Likely to Stay There as Adults
Chances of moving up or down the family income ladder, by parents' quintile

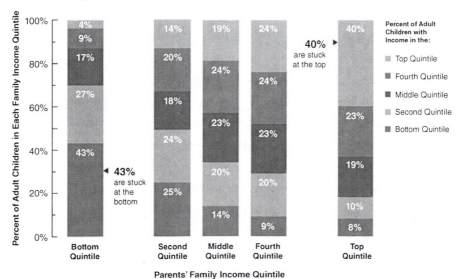

Note: Numbers are adjusted for family size.

Translated: classes tend to reproduce themselves. The greatest predictor of one's class position as an adult is the class position of one's parents. Hard work, persistence, courage, and other personal facts will certainly play a role in your life path. But sociology tells us with great precision and credibility that forces mostly beyond your control will play as large but probably a larger role in shaping your outcomes. What types of forces? Simple facts such as:

- Gender
- Family size and structure
- Race
- Country of birth
- Year of birth
- Wartime or peacetime
- Availability of quality health care
- Supply of good education

And on and on. This list could easily include hundreds of variables, virtually none of which are within the control of the individual.

Change any one of these factors and you and I would be different people. Our life outcomes would be entirely new. Change two or more factors and the differences combine and multiply to produce a life totally unrecognizable from the one you now call your own. If one is fortunate enough to be learning about sociology at the university level, odds are this change would be in a negative direction. Attending college already puts one in a very elite group of human beings. Less than 7% of the world's population has any university education.[66]

Recognizing that you could have just easily been born in North Korea, or during the Civil War, or as a child soldier in Uganda, or simply one of the 47 million below the U.S. poverty line induces an immediate interest in the welfare of those people. Coming to terms with the real possibility of an alternate life in which I am not the person considering how to help but indeed the person who needs the help nearly instantly opens one's heart. As President Obama said when learning of the shooting death of Trayvon Martin, "I could have been him." Had one or two variables been dialed in differently for Barack

Obama, he would not have ended up at Harvard Law but perhaps the victim of a vigilante attack. And a version of that is true for all of us.

Sociology is often derided for being a depressing discipline, second only to economics, the original "dismal science," through its admittedly myopic focus on social problems and injustice. As one clever undergraduate recalled to me, "It's like a whole semester of the nightly news without the sports at the end to cheer me up." On the whole, the field could afford to be a little deliberately brighter, highlighting the many signs of progress and encouraging advances around the world. But there's a case to be made, too, for the role of sociology as a kind of cultural prophet, in the original, Old Testament sense of the word. The prophet was the one who held up a mirror to the society, and warned what would come if changes were not made. Prophets such as Jeremiah, Isaiah, and Daniel often spoke to the wider public and to leaders of the society, and sometimes were kept as loyal advisors to kings and priests. Their motive was always to try to continually align the society with its highest values and greatest promise. In a sense, they served as the personified conscience of the culture.

Sociology's role as prophet or conscience to the broader society could not be more needed today. iCulture is effectively Id on steroids; unrestrained desire, egoistic, pleasure seeking, and generally seeing others as objects. In this context, something like a superego is not only helpful, but is also a matter of cultural survival. Even it means that sociology might have to develop an unpleasant reputation as a "downer," (particularly to college students), it will have to be seen as an acceptable occupational hazard.

Each semester, I end my Intro class with a lecture based on the ideas in this book. In it, I describe what I call "the spiritual gifts of sociology." At the conclusion of the lecture one semester, a male student approached with tears in his eyes. He said that these words were exactly what he needed to hear. "I had no idea how selfish I had become. I was headed down a path to becoming the very person I hated. You woke me up to how people need me; that my problems are so small compared to theirs." I gave him a hug and asked him not to be too hard on himself. I also encouraged him to use the energy of this moment to think about which issue or group he most wanted to help. Later he came back and said that gender injustice was it. "Why that one?," I enquired. "Because that where I need the most help," he said.

Learning about the many forms of injustice in the world and how they came to be is not only an invitation to help undo them. It is also an opportunity to undo the lack of virtue in ourselves, the lack of spiritual maturity we all need to address. Sociology shows us the connections between the problems out there and our role in perpetuating them. No longer can we simply dismiss them as having nothing to do with us, that they are as remote and hopeless as a sandstorm on Mars. Only the field of sociology has the power to persuasively point out the link between my actions and the injustices we hear about from the other side of the world. Whereas iCulture lets us off the hook and distracts us from reality with sparkly pleasures, social science yanks us back, knocks the scales off our eyes, and gently asks, "What are you going to do?" Put simply, sociology can lead us from the dead end of apathy to the journey of empathy. And empathy is the only thing that has ever saved us.

The benefits of cultivating empathy and the other virtues is simply too great and important to pass by. Learning about the depth and difficulty of the social challenges we face as a nation and world increases the possibility of caring for others as extensions of ourselves, as Aristotle wrote. It increases the chances for connecting and bonding with people very different from ourselves, thereby decreasing the likelihood of violence and war. As we see our sister or father in the stories of injustice told by sociologists, our humanity grows. Our soul reaches to meet theirs. This is the essence of virtue. It is also, miraculously, the heart of spirituality.

Humility

For many decades, social psychologists have been aware of the phenomenon known as *primus inter pares* or illusory superiority. For lovers of Garrison Keillor, it is also known informally as the "Lake Wobegon effect." This common cognitive fallacy assumes that oneself and members of one's group are naturally superior and thereby unlike all others. This is frequently encountered in terms of driving ability, ethical judgment, and resistance to group influence.

A common version seen in sociology is the estimated effect of advertising. A majority of Americans each year since the 1970s have stated that while they are certain advertising has an enormous influence on others ("the average person") it has little to no effect on themselves. Clearly this is not only logically impossible, but also violates the principles of mathematics. Someone is buying all those selfie sticks and jeggings, but everyone thinks it's the other guy, not them.

Sociology dismantles illusory superiority by confronting us with the truth of our own inescapable averageness. This is not the same as you are not special or valuable. Far from it. It simply states the truth that on the whole, we are more like others than we are different, and more to the point, more like them than we like to believe. The net result is humbling.

A key lesson picked up during any adequate Intro to Sociology class is that many of my accomplishments are not because of my effort. As mentioned above, had it not been for a fortuitous collection of accidents of birth, my life might be much more difficult but certainly very different than it currently is. In addition to fostering empathy, this knowledge takes the puff out of one's chest almost immediately.

For example, many college students are proud of their being admitted to the school they attend. They feel they genuinely deserve it. It is a result of tenacity, hard work, practice, high achievement, and talent. So far so good. Further questions remain, however. Who is paying for this education? Odds are you are in the 80% of college students who work part-time while in college, but not to pay for college but merely for extra spending money. Only 18% of American college students pay their way through college.[67] Most college students rely on some type of financial aid, largely federal loans, to pay for college. These loans have low interest rates and may be paid off over the course of several decades. Most importantly, they are a creation of the federal government only since 1965. Had you been born prior to that date or in less developed country, access to higher education would be well out of reach.

Sociology tells us, too, that access to higher education is not merely the result of finding the funds and meeting the admission requirements. It is also deeply tied to the type and quality of education you have already received, both in primary and secondary school. To a very large degree, one's chances of doing well in high school, having a high GPA, good SAT scores, being involved in extracurricular activities, and being able to write an impressive entrance essay are a result of the resources of your local school. And the sociology of education is very clear about where these resources come from: (1) local tax revenue and (2) parent's tuition. If "parent's tuition" is a meaningless phrase to you, that means you were one of the 90% of U.S. students who attended a public high school. This means that most of your school's funding came from taxes collected through a school district tax. These taxes are levied based on the appraised value of residential and commercial properties, mostly. The higher the property value, the more money is generated for the school. This therefore ties school resources directly to the wealth or poverty of the surrounding area. In a phrase, poor neighborhood = poor school.

Social research can help us here. In 2010, low-poverty schools had a high school graduation rate of 91%. The rate for high poverty schools was only 68%.[68] The message could not be more clear: the chances of me receiving a quality education and attending college are already structured by what school I happen to attend. Most Americans do not have the ability to move wherever they like to attend school. They attend the school in their neighborhood. If that school happens to be in a high poverty area, that school is likely to be underperforming and my educational future is limited.

Humility begins to sink in upon learning such facts. Add to this the harsh irony that education is held as precisely *the pathway* out of poverty and up the socioeconomic ladder. But as long as educational quality is tied to neighborhood resources, this is merely a cruel joke.

For those who attended private schools or whose parents are paying for most or all of college expenses, the depth of humility must be proportionately greater. We are all standing on the shoulders of very generous giants. We should make the most of the blessings and good fortune bestowed on us through no effort by us. If we wish to cling to the Myth of Deserve, we will come up short on this score.

Humility in the age of iCulture is crucial for another, very important psychological and spiritual reason. Humility is a powerful antidote to narcissism, the spiritual epidemic of the 21st century. Erich Fromm, the eminent American psychologist and author of the beautiful *The Art of Loving*, describes how damaging narcissism can be both to oneself and to others:

> "The main condition for the achievement of love is the overcoming of one's narcissism. The narcissistic orientation is one in which one experiences as real only that which exists within oneself, while the phenomena in the outside world have no reality in themselves, but are experienced only from the viewpoint of their being useful or dangerous to one."[69]

The myth of independent accomplishment and the practice of self-worship crumbles under the onslaught of sociological facts. For we are none of us truly independent, our achievements are actually collaborations, and the self is a social performance. What is left to worship? Only the miracle of Creation, the grace and blessings we have received, and the opportunity to live itself. We are then left with an abundance of humble feelings and the urge to give back to those many who make our lives and happiness possible.

Gratitude

The sister of humility is gratitude. The feeling of thankfulness often flows to fill the place held by pride and vanity. Gratitude as a sensation is proof positive of Aristotle's argument regarding eudaimonia. It is a feeling of fullness, of satisfaction and contentment. One is not only aware of one's blessings and gifts, but happy about them. Brother David Steindl-Rast, the beloved Austrian Catholic monk, has built his entire spiritual approach around gratitude, which he considers the pure essence of spirituality. "Look closely and you will find that people are happy because they are grateful. The opposite of gratefulness is just taking everything for granted."[70] Implicit in his remark is the centrality of mindfulness, again the gateway to all spiritual growth and the first gift of sociology.

Regular contact with sociological data and social theory seem to foster an appreciation for the lot one has been dealt. I know of exactly zero cases in which more sociology has resulted in less gratitude, more greed, increased envy, or lower satisfaction. This is likely the opposite of the experience students have in business, economics, or athletics. In these fields, one is subtly encouraged to be in a perpetual state of comparison, always looking over one's shoulder to see how the other guy is doing and try to catch up to them if they are ahead (and someone always is). Competition is the master attitude of these fields, which is why they synch with mainstream American culture so smoothly and sociology so poorly.

The gift of gratitude is one of the major ways by which sociology's unfortunate reputation as a "downer" discipline is offset. It is difficult to hear day after day about the panoply of devastating problems the world faces. But for most listeners, this litany of lamentations is accompanied by the gentle presence of thankfulness. Even if one's life is currently in tatters, a perspective on the greater suffering of others somehow puts one's personal misery on the shelf for at least a moment. It allows one to appreciate that at least you have tatters. If sociology encourages a type of comparison like the fields above, its effect is in the opposite direction. It nurtures a healthy self-love and a sense that life is pretty okay after all. The positive mental and emotional effects of felt gratitude are powerful and well-documented.[71] Eudaimonia is being planted.

More importantly, mindfulness and gratitude of this sort underscore the sociological fact of the immeasurable dependency we have on countless others. An exercise we often do when I teach about Marx's labor theory of value is to hold up a simple water bottle. I then ask the students, "Where does this come from?" After sorting through a number of initial smarty-pants replies ("7–11!" "The ground!" "Your mom's house"!), we then track the stages in the process from underground water to sealed bottle in my hand in Texas. At every step, dozens of human beings, their creativity, energy, labor, dedication, and sacrifice were essential. By the time the bottle ends up in my hand, hundreds of separate human lives have been involved. At that's just for a measly bottle of Ozarka. We then repeat the exercise on objects the students brought with them: backpacks, food, smartphones (these are the best), and so on. Then we move on to talk about the classroom we are in, the building we are in, the landscaping outside, the electricity and water that make it all happen, the safe streets near campus, the banks that financed their loans, etc. Now we are talking about easily tens of thousands of totally anonymous human beings who work together each day, many of them with insufficient compensation, to bring the world we take for granted into being for us. As I ask them about their thoughts and feelings about these facts, I invariably hear things like: dependency, awareness, surprise, and more than any other: appreciation.

We live in a massive web of interdependency. Sociology is the discipline most able to make this fact crystal clear. Our methods, particularly network analysis, reveal the structure of these connections with unrivaled transparency. Our theories provide compelling explanations of the processes behind this web and its effects on people and systems. And when engaged mindfully, sociology nurtures the heart of gratitude that is essential for deep happiness, the aim of virtue and the fruit of spiritual practice.

Openness

It is axiomatic today to say that we lived in a globalized world. It is a statement that is as true as it is meaningless if not interpreted properly. In a sense, humans have long lived in a globalized world. Civilizations such as the Sumerians were trading with the ancient Egyptians and Indians thousands of years before the discovery of North America. What distinguishes modern globalization is the speed of exchange, scope of diversity, and durability of contact. Never before have humans been able to buy and sell goods from the other side of the planet and potentially have them delivered the same day. And not only from far away, but from dozens of faraway societies. If one prefers foreign wine, for example, one will have to specify South African, New Zealand, French, Portuguese, or Dutch.

The extension of this fact to culture is even more dramatic. The most obvious effect for college students (and professors) is in the classroom. When I began teaching at the university level in 1997, about one student in 20 would be from a foreign country. Typically these were British or Indian. Recently one of my sections of Intro to Sociology was 50% foreign students, most of them first-generation college students. The list of countries of origin was stunning: Indonesia, Pakistan, Sri Lanka, Singapore, Syria, Ireland, Denmark, Mexico, and even Kansas.

These students were mixed in with the standard supply of Texans. For both, this was their longest period of exposure to people from other lands. They learned much from each other, they told me. But the most important thing they learned is that their particular way of doing things, long accepted as The Only Way, is but one way among thousands. Perhaps they had heard of these differences before, such as fasting during Ramadan or open display of affection between males, but had never actually seen and heard it in person. Everything changes when you actually know the name, face, and voice of a real human being who embodies all the differences you've only heard about before.

Sociological research tells us that such encounters are quite rare, actually. Humans prefer homophily, the desire to be with those who resemble ourselves, according to sociologists such as Miller McPherson and Nicholas Christakis. We cluster on the basis of similarity, whether it be religion, race, economic class, or political tastes. But another gift of university—when done properly—is that it encourages mixing across these categories. Required classes are without question one of the most effective mechanisms by which this occurs. Introductory Sociology classes are frequently in this category and with intentional design and effort, can be extraordinary laboratories for discovering the beauty of difference.

These lessons are at least as important as the particular knowledge of skill being imparted academically. For the deeper truth about globalization is that it is permanent and irreversible. The world is only getting smaller. We cannot know much about the future with precision, but one thing we can know with certainty is that getting along with an unprecedented diversity of other people will be essential. At least as long as survival is something we care about. Isolation, fundamentalism, and xenophobia have well-documented and reliable effects: hatred, violence, war, and genocide. As sociologist Peter Berger observes in his work on secularization, the central "ism" of the future will be pluralism. Pluralism is the coexistence of multiple different cultures within a system. This is not only an accurate description of the lived experience of globalization; it is also in my view the only sustainable condition for future human societies.

Among the virtues, pluralism is most akin to moderation, the result of what Aristotle called the "golden mean," or the balance point between two extremes. Moderation per se conveys more an evaluative dimension than I mean with openness. Openness, I would offer, is prerequisite for moderation. Without the ability to hear all perspectives, moderation between them cannot occur. Openness, therefore, also contains a significant portion of humility, as one must be sufficiently modest about the correctness or finality of one's views and actions in order to truly hear and understand those of others.

Openness does not, however, imply a lack of convictions or mushy moral code. It does not do away with sound ethical judgment or "practical wisdom" as virtue ethicists call it. Openness merely means a concerted effort to suspend biases and preferences, to remain respectful and curious about new and different ways of living or interpreting a situation. One is always free to conclude that the new way is bollocks. But the virtue of openness demands that we never begin with that posture.

The standard methods of sociology are actually preinstalled with virtual mandates for openness. In the early days of sociology, the field was often allied with anthropology, both intellectually and organizationally. Anthropologists deal with diverse human cultures as their primary interest, so the concept of openness quickly became an occupational necessity. The scientific term invented by Franz Boas to refer to this methodological openness was "cultural relativism." Boas meant with this term that cultural forms and practices should only be interpreted and evaluated by the norms and values of that particular culture. If one fails to do this, cultural differences quickly degrade into cultural judgments, what anthropologists call "ethnocentrism." Cultural relativism and ethnocentrism have been imported into sociology and prove especially useful in qualitative research, such as participant observation and interviews.

A lack of cultural relativism in the sociology of religion can be disastrous. Imagine a researcher who surveyed 2,000 religious people on their views of Jesus Christ. She compiles and analyzes the data, and then ranks them in order of their "Biblical correctness." Latter Day Saints receive, according to her estimation, last place in the ranking due to their Book of Mormon, which she regards as "apostate," while the Assembly of God is given first place, owing to their strict biblical literalism and spirited rituals. In the footnotes, the author thanks her local AOG church, where she is a member, for their support. She should probably also apply for a job at this church, as her days in sociology are numbered.

Sociology is not the only discipline that can cultivate the virtue of openness. History, literature, psychology (to a degree), and of course anthropology are effective agents as well. But sociology has a few advantages. First, our field can better than most reveal and describe the enormous diversity *within* a society, primarily through survey and demographic research. Anthropology is particularly well-suited for understanding diversity across societies and these differences in exhaustive detail (e.g. Saramacca of South America vs. Mbuti of Africa). But how to grasp the subtle distinctions between a middle age Catholic female from Portland who believes that Pope Francis is the anti-Christ in disguise and a young female from Dallas who recently returned to Catholicism due to her love for Papa Frankie? This is the kind of day-to-day diversity that most regular people need help with. Not only by understanding the sociological roots of such puzzles, but by encouraging, through empathy, a deeper insight into their perception of the world. Such a practice will gradually open the mind, challenge prejudices, and reduce blockages to connection.

Second, sociology is oriented to the group level, providing a needed complement to psychology's individual focus. Psychology is useful at helping us understand why Nick said or did a thing, but not why people like Nick (from his demographic and cultural groups) do similar things in reliable ways. Psychology also has a powerful clinical component that is attached at present to identifying disorders, which often produce stigma and a stunning lack of openness. History as a discipline is the silver medal winner in promoting openness, actually. Like sociology, history has a macro-level focus, uses comparison heavily, and is famous for its exhaustive detail in description. As such, history demands a consistently open mind; open to enormous diversity within the story of one society, and open to learning about many other cultures to better understand the one being examined. The limitation of history with respect to openness is its lack of present-day orientation. While it is true that wise living in the present can only be achieved with a full grasp of the past, a solitary focus on the past mires one there. The result is an inability to be relevant and useful for today's problems. Sociology offers a needed balance here: a knowledge and appreciation of the past alongside a full array of tools and ideas for making sense of the present. However, when sociology loses a historical perspective, as it has in recent years, it becomes excessively fixed in the present and is crippled in its ability to deliver adequate explanations and solutions. This is effectively a loss of openness to the past.

On a daily basis, the virtue of openness is the most useful for regular people living in the 21st century. At the root of many of today's most vexing problems are various forms of closedness. Sexism is the refusal to be open to the idea of equality between the genders. Racism is being closed to those with different skin. Tribalism is a rampant version, wherein a group is not open to the possibility of other groups being equal or even worthwhile compared to theirs. Many of our toughest socioeconomic problems result from a closed mind to policies and values that would improve the lives of millions, as they have in other countries. The rigid resistance to new ideas in order to show loyalty to tradition or merely because of comfort is unsustainable in a globalized, pluralistic reality. It is in fact merely a slow path to fanaticism and violence on the societal level, bigotry and stagnation on the individual level. In sum, our personal and collective lives will be closer to eudaimonia through the virtue of openness.

J. Krisnamurti summarized well the spiritual fruits of this truth: "The ability to observe without evaluating is the highest form of intelligence." Admittedly, this task is easier said than done. But sociological life is a spiritual discipline of the highest rigor in developing the open mind. The open mind is the gateway to the open heart, which leads to real and abiding happiness.

Justice

Ask 10 sociologists why the entered the field. Eleven of them will say "to improve the world," or some variation thereof.

It is widely known that sociologists have a bent toward social activism. For some, this inclination is an unvarnished good, lending scientific precision and rigor to ameliorating the woes of the world. For others, it is an unfortunate politicizing of pure intellectual discovery that often does more harm than good. This latter position is perplexing to me. It implies that all the other branches of science—biology, chemistry, psychology, meteorology, etc.—are apolitical or lack normative dimensions. It suggests that science is a pure method for discovering facts and/or the information produced by that process. The view conjures an image of an expressionless robot pouring chemicals from beaker to beaker or measuring insects and recording observations. This is the Spock version of science. It also has absolutely no relationship to actual human science in the present day.

Science, as intimated in previous sections, is not and cannot be made immune from the natures of the humans who inescapably practice it. That nature is intrinsically emotional, moral, and most importantly, irrational. Yes, we certainly are rational (in part), but one of the first lessons of social science is that we are far from perfectly rational, and that's a good thing. Our irrationality is what makes us altruistic, sensual, artistic, and endearing. This is not an invitation to the kind of wild irrationality that says the earth is 6,000 years old or that disease is caused by past bad behavior. But it is an embrace of the mild irrationality that allows emotion and moral sentiments to influence logic. That's how we are built, and it's a gift. If not for this, we'd have no Sam Cooke and *Lord of the Rings*, and that's hardly a world worth living in.

Sociology is simply more honest about its normative leanings and accepting of emotion than other sciences. On the whole, those leanings and emotions center on the idea of justice. Social justice can be defined as the interest in equality in economic, political, and cultural sectors of life. Those advocating social justice might support a minimum wage that is linked to the cost of living in a region. They might argue against policies that replace human workers with mechanization, such as drones or automated tellers. Social justice allies would generally oppose war but might support the use of the military to deliver and protect humanitarian aid. Equality of opportunity as well as equality of outcome (as close as can be achieved) is the characteristic concern of justice allies, and sociological research confronts one constantly with how poorly these goals are being met. Sociologists and sociology students are typically wading knee deep in data describing in full detail the extent of our various failures in equality. A senior sociology major once told me that she knew she was a legitimate sociologist when she could offer from memory the child poverty rate in Texas and compare it with three other states. She described such drilled-in factoids as "ammo in my belt."

Armed with such data and with years of outrageous stories of injustice sloshing about in their noggins, sociology students are among the best and most ardent advocates for equality and social change. However, it has come to come my attention recently—thanks to my hip and attentive undergrads—that there is a phrase used on the Internet to refer to such people: the SJW: "Social Justice Warrior." The phrase is deployed as a put down, normally suggesting that the "warrior" is not sincere about their beliefs nor well-informed. In other words, being a SJW is merely a way to *appear* as though one cares, knows about, and plans to do something about the issue. It's a performance a la Goffman's dramaturgy. In this case, though, it is always a bad performance, a poor front. In fact, in some circles it is impossible to take a position for social justice that is perceived as authentic— even if you just got back from three years lobbying for the issue on Capitol Hill. This is because the SJW label has become so viral that it has contaminated all potential attempts at public justice advocacy. To speak up for social justice is to be a SJW, at which point one's credibility evaporates and mocking is the only reply.

This development illustrates the desperate need for true justice advocates in the current culture. Advocates who are not armed with Wikipedia lines or You-Tube quotes, but time-tested, rigorously analyzed data that conveys expertise and sincerity. Such justice activists are just that: active. They put their bodies and time where their mouth is, whether it be in the form or research, campaigning, volunteering, donating, educating, or running for office. In so doing, they cease to be caricatures of do-gooders seeking only the reputational points from friends, but people those friends actually aspire to be like, local versions of Dolores de la Huerta, Harvey Milk, Pete Seeger, and Aung San Suu Kyi.

But one need not wait for a global stage and giant issues such as national liberation to get involved. Every person lives within a sphere of influence where they can be a powerful force for justice. If the web of interdependence is true, then every act in the direction of virtue and equality has reverberating effects the full extent of which we may never know. As I tell my students on the last day of class, you will change the world. Just by being alive and touching the lives of others you make an impact. Even the tiniest pebble causes waves that reach to the shore. The only questions are what type and how much.

A recent example of a marvelous form of small-scale activism was conveyed by my students but made possible by social media. The comment-sharing app known as Yik-Yak is absurdly popular on college campuses. Due to the anonymous nature of posts, an abnormally large amount of normally socially inappropriate remarks are made. According to a male sophomore student, a heated exchange about racism ensued after the shooting of Trayvon Martin. The originally poster insisted that "Racism is only a thing because we won't stop talking about it." Dozens of replies followed, some in agreement, some not. So far pretty predictable. But then, said this student, one brave soul posted, "HAVEN'T YOU EVER HEARD OF INSTITUTIONAL RACISM? TAKE A SOCIOLOGY CLASS!!" This amazing post was followed by several spelling out exactly what institutional racism was, how it differed from garden-variety individual racism, and how this was the type we need to be looking for and trying to get rid of. Sociology, they argued, was the main way to learn about the true nature and extent of modern racism.

I've never been more proud.

Whether or not any of those were my students is irrelevant. They were some sociologists' students, and they were representing the discipline in fine fashion. They were being positive forces for justice in the small sphere of influence they inhabited and could control. These students could have ignored the remark or watched the fray as a spectator sport. But they couldn't. Instead, they acted. They used this snarky cowardly app as a space for micro-activism. Because they knew better, they could do better.

If this happened on one day on my campus, I can only assume that it is happening every day on every campus in some fashion. But not just in these contexts. Any encounter, real or virtual, is a potential space for this type of micro-activism. Merely standing up with better information and a bigger heart.

Not in a condescending or confrontational way, but simply being present with what you have. The objective is simply to not allow false, ignorant, or hurtful perspectives to go unchallenged.

Without sociology, these micro-activists might still have engaged, still have argued ably for their view, and maybe changed a few minds. But with sociology, they are much better equipped and more likely to be effective. It's the difference between taking a knife to a gunfight and taking a lightsaber to a gunfight.

As briefly mentioned above, sociology is one of the few academic disciplines that actually fosters eudaimonia, a durable happiness. Therapists have a useful phrase to describe the way many other fields operate: "Compare leads to despair." Business, for example, both in its academic form and applied form, are premised on competition, which is simply an aggressive mode of comparison. In business, students and practitioners are marinated for years in a slow cooker of competition. They learn not only that it is good, but natural. Other ways of living life, organizing society, or treating people are hardly imaginable. Competition is natural, of course, but no more natural or primary than cooperation. Sociology teaches students and professionals that comparison is useful, too, but in a very different way. It is comparison with an eye to helping the other if they are in a lesser position, or equalizing the gap between the other and myself. Here, competition takes a back seat to cooperation and connection. In this respect, sociology generally resists the powerful impulse toward objectification that modernity has nearly perfected. Human beings are not instruments for use, either for profit, pleasure, or oppression. We have more work to do in this area to be a match for these overwhelming forces of objectification. But sociology, along with spiritual traditions and humanitarian organizations are among the greatest sources of promise for insisting on the inherent dignity of persons.

EPILOGUE
Conscience & Causes

Four and a half minutes.

That's the elapsed time between when I told my mom I had bought my first house and her reminding me I needed to take my boxes of old scrapbooks and nostalgia out of her house. I had agreed to do this a long time ago, so it was not that big a deal. And she obviously wanted it out—pronto. What struck me, though, was how much of it there was. I had clung to every fragment of my adolescence. It looked like an intervention from *Hoarders*.

In among the dusty cardboard boxes, was a newspaper clipping about my graduation from high school. It was customary among small Texas towns to publish the names and photos of the senior class, along with a little statement from the graduate about their plans for future. After shaking my head over all the hair I had and the narrow smirking face hiding behind huge Sally Jesse Raphael-style glasses, I noticed the statement I had submitted:

"Goal: To fight for lost causes, because they are the only ones worth fighting for."

More than two decades later, the prescience of that half-baked comment is giving me the chills. This book itself can be seen as the most recent lost cause. Sociologists on the whole are not known for their interest in spirituality. Likewise, spiritual types are hard to find at ASA. Writing a book about their common themes might as well be a heading on the Wiki page for Lost Causes.

But even somehow at 18 plucky years of age, I was drawn to hard problems and unpopular topics. Not because they kept me entertained or could make me famous, but just because no one else seemed to want to. And because it appeared to me then, in my peak of idealistic fervor, that these issues were desperately important but folks had just given up. They were "lost causes" because other people had gotten lost working on them. There was a feeling of sadness and defeat in the phrase, a sense of Don Quixote about it all. Adults, I figured, had tried and failed due mainly to their being adults, not a kid like me. My generation had new energy and innovation that the Baby Boomers had wasted on Woodstock and Quaaludes. We—especially me—were the upgrade. We were America 2.0. Lost causes would finally be found.

Since then I and other Gen Xers have been busy tilting at windmills, too, with varying degrees of success. One of the first lost causes I got involved in was improving the lives of the poor in Texas. For six years, I worked alongside some of the brightest policy minds in our state to at least make sure that the bad bills didn't become law. Sometimes we even helped get good things passed, such as the Children's Health Insurance Program (CHIP) and increases in monthly cash aid to the poor. The most extreme of lost causes I worked on was for the creation of a state income tax. To convey a sense of how popular this idea was, a colleague took me for a visit to the nearby Texas State Cemetery. He showed the tombstone of a long-serving Texas Representative. On it was etched, "He tried to pass a tax bill."

Upon reflection I realized my early interest in lost causes was nurtured along at every by step by those trained in the social sciences. In high school it was Marshall Galvez, the history teacher from New Orleans who introduced me to effective argumentation and the depths of Southern social problems. In college it was a remarkable group of professors and mentors, mainly sociologists and journalists. Ed Kain, Maria Lowe, and Dan Hilliard fanned the flames of social activism through their inspiring classes on the family, methods, and cultural theory. Glen McClish, the rhetorician, showed me the power of the written word to change history in a positive direction. And Sybil Hampton, one of the original Little Rock Nine, mentored me in the need for humility and perseverance when working on a lost cause. In journalism school it was the firm but gentle Horace Newcomb who helped me understand how social research can be a formidable tool for social reform. Alongside these flesh-and-blood mentors were virtual guides whose books during the doctoral years pushed my thinking in new ways and opened me to a huge array of lost causes to get lost in. These included Neil Postman, Herbert Gans, Barbara Ehrenreich, William Julius Wilson, Noam Chomsky, bell hooks, and most of all, Paulo Freire. Through their writing my consciousness was expanded, but more importantly my *conscience* was expanded.

Joining these guides from academia were a series of mentors from the realm of spirituality and religion. In college it was Fr. Bob Scott who helped me for the first time see that "God loves us and wants us to be happy." In journalism school I befriended the Austin civil rights legend Jim Harrington who blended scripture with Marx in his eloquent conversations with me. While doing my graduate work in sociology, I needed new and very potent forms of spirituality to stay sane and balanced. This came in the form of Joseph Campbell, Fr. Thomas Keating, Hafiz, Jack Kornfield, and the great Alan Watts. At no point did I feel the slightest tension between what I was learning in social science and what I was learning from the spiritual traditions. In fact, just the opposite. This book is a chronicle of the many common revelations and gifts I found in both.

Another major reason for writing this book was to honor these social scientists and spiritual teachers for widening my conscience. I wasn't aware at the time, of course, that it needed widening. I thought I was a pretty good person, and indeed probably was in a conventional sense. The problem was that I had a narrow (traditional) idea of what being good meant. It was mainly defined in the negative; what I didn't do. I didn't steal, kill, dishonor my parents, hurt people intentionally, or break the law. I also did my best not to act in a way that conflicted with my inner moral compass. So far, so good. The dirty trick that sociology pulled was *to redefine the directions on the compass*. It changed the boundaries of goodness, what I have come to call my "moral jurisdiction." After sociology, the limits of my action were no longer confined to my family, friends, and tribe. The human community was my tribe. And it wasn't just the bad things I didn't do that mattered, but also the enormous amount of newly discovered good that I wasn't doing! After a brief self-esteem crisis, I began to recalibrate my life in line with this new compass. As the adage says, "Once he knew better, he could do better." This continues to the present day.

I believe I speak for thousands of others who can tell a similar story. I personally know of dozens who have voiced parallel accounts from their own lives. Sociology has a distinct yet sneaky way of blowing your mind while growing your heart. As I've argued here, sociology is a beautiful and challenging spiritual practice. It helps us know the self but see how foolish selfishness is. It shows us the inherent connection between us and others, plus how and why to care for them. It reveals the miracle of the human world, inspiring us with hope and filling us with wonder. It gives us the tools to find the truth and the courage to speak it. It cultivates virtues essential for a flourishing life. My aim in this book has been to demonstrate exactly how these work and how urgently needed they are in the world. There is one more important spiritual gift of sociology, however, one that is most needed on college campuses, but definitely in the broader world as well.

The number one problem students bring to my office is a feeling of no purpose. Over the years, hundreds have voiced a version of this feeling. It is described as an emptiness, a lack of direction or focus, an absence of inspiration or passion. Though their lives may be free of any serious trauma, conflict, or obstacle, and they may appear on the surface very happy, inside a gnawing void is haunting them. My colleague Paul Froese has written a marvelous book about this issue, *On Purpose*, showing how the meaning one gives life is a social process, and that purpose is a prerequisite for human well-being. He makes clear in the book that the purpose problem extends far beyond my office, and is perhaps *the* problem of modern life.

Each time I am both disturbed and pleased to hear of this trouble from undergraduates. Disturbed because their suffering is real. Anomie is not a fun place to live. It has a way of making sensible people desperate, leading to bad decisions. It also turns shrewd people highly suggestible, causing them to cling to any old purpose that comes along, or switching between many in a frantic search for sure footing, which invariably wastes precious time. All of these are painful, needless, and ought be avoided. But I am pleased when they speak to me about lack of purpose because they have come to the right place. Sociology is a purpose distribution center.

There is no better purpose than one that uses your talents to improve the world. Few students have a poverty of talent. They merely have a poverty of ideas for how to use their talent. If one is skilled with numbers, sociology offers countless (pun intended) avenues to use that talent to conduct quantitative social research which could help society better understand the scope of it challenges and how best to address them. If one has a gift with words, sociology has no end of work for you, crafting articles, laws, policies, speeches, lectures, and even books like this one. If one is good with people, sociology is the home for you. We need folks who are effective at relating to others to conduct interviews, hold focus groups, run experiments, supervise observations, and translate to the broader public. If your talents lie elsewhere, have no fear; sociology will give you a target for your gifts. That target, it turns out, is always the same: telling the truth to help people.

The world is busy each day, it seems, creating problems while we are busy solving them. There is no shortage of challenges for us to tackle. But there is actually a shortage of people telling the truth about the world and its problems, and an extreme shortage of those passionate about fixing them. The world needs sociologically minded people passionately telling the truth in order to fix problems. The first spiritual gift of sociology, of course, is mindfulness; thus, the first duty of the sociologically minded is not make it any worse, a kind of Hippocratic Oath for the Community. An immediate and simple purpose is to pledge, in the spirit of the Bodhisattva vow, to try in every way to reduce the suffering of the world by not participating in those actions that add to the litany of problems. This may mean something as simple as not wasting water, refusing to patronize businesses that treat workers poorly, or consuming media that degrade human dignity. Creativity in this area is encouraged. This purpose, if practiced by enough people, would go a long way to decreasing the social problems we face, and anyone can do it.

But probably the most satisfying way to find purpose is to mindfully and carefully consider how you spend your time. As Mumford and Sons say in their song "Awake My Soul," "Where you invest your love, you invest your life." This may mean your choice of vocation, past times, friends, university, or romantic partner. Each of these will invariably consume a huge chunk of your time and your "love" in the form of passion and energy. As such, they should be considered sites of spiritual practice. Contrary to popular misunderstandings, spirituality is not and has never been confined to holy places or solitary meditation. Indeed the central assumption of this book is that every dimension of life, including sociology (or any other field), can be made a location of profound spiritual growth and discovery.

For most of us, our work is the place we spend the bulk of our time. It is therefore the place where we are most likely to find purpose, or, if less mindful, not find it. I humbly submit that when considering a vocation, allow sociology to advise your choice. Be open to its spiritual gifts: justice, mindfulness, humility, and empathy. Let them shape your thinking about purpose. Consider questions that include a spiritual and ethical dimension. What do I want to leave behind? What do I want to be known for? How can I use my unique bag of talents to help? Who do I feel called to serve? The culture we inhabit does not encourage these questions and even considers them absurd. It will likely not even tolerate the topic of purpose as there is no profit in purpose. Instead it urges criteria such as money, prestige, and practicality.

The culture will push you to give your life to cash and career. I ask that you give it to a cause. Preferably a "lost" one.

But as a plucky young man once said, lost causes are the only ones worth fighting for.

Notes

1 Polkinghorne, J. C. (2007). *Exploring reality: The intertwining of science and religion* (No. 65). New Haven: Yale University Press.

2 Gould, S. J. (1997). Nonoverlapping Magisteria. *Natural History* 106 (March): 16–22.

3 Wilber, K. (2001). *Quantum questions: mystical writings of the world's greatest physicists.* Boston: Shambhala.

4 Collins, F. (2006). *The language of God: A scientist presents evidence for belief.* New York, NY: Free Press.

5 Harris, S. (2014). *Waking up: A guide to spirituality without religion.* New York, NY: Simon and Schuster

6 James, W. (1985). *The varieties of religious experience.* Cambridge, MA: Harvard University Press.

7 Tipler, F. (1994). *The physics of immortality: Modern cosmology, God, and the resurrection of the dead.* New York, NY: Doubleday.

8 Nickell, J. (2013). *The Science of miracles: Investigating the incredible.* Amherst, NY: Prometheus Books.

9 Berger, P. (1967). *The sacred canopy: Elements of a sociological theory of religion.* Garden City, NY: Doubleday.

10 Cooley, C. H. (1902). *The looking-glass self.* O'Brien, 126–128.

11 Mead, G., & Morris, C. (1934). *Mind, self and society from the standpoint of a social behaviorist.* Chicago, IL: University of Chicago Press.

12 Goffman, E. (1973). *The presentation of self in everyday life.* Woodstock, NY: Overlook Press.

13 Shakespeare, W. (1954). *As you like it* (Rev. ed.). New Haven, CT: Yale University Press.

14 Butler, J. (1994). Gender as performance: An interview with Judith Butler. *Radical Philosophy, 67*(1), 32–39.

15 Lorber, J., & Farrell, S. A. (Eds.). (1991). *The social construction of gender.* Newbury Park, CA: SAGE publications.

16 Fausto-Sterling, A. (2012). *Sex/gender: Biology in a social world.* New York: Routledge.

17 Berthiaume, A. (1996). Les petits caractères. *XYZ. La revue de la nouvelle*, (48), 36–38.

18 Bauman, Z. (2000). *Liquid modernity.* Cambridge, UK: Polity Press.

19 Eckersley, R. (2006). Is modern Western culture a health hazard? *International journal of epidemiology, 35*(2), 252–258

20 Ibid, pp. 257

21 Tillich, P., & Church, F. F. (1999). *The essential Tillich*. Chicago: University of Chicago Press.

22 Loy, D. (1996). Beyond good and evil? A buddhist critique of Nietzsche. *Asian Philosophy, 6*(1), 37–57.

23 Brown, D. (1991). *Human universals*. Philadelphia, PA: Temple University Press.

24 Douglas, M. (1966). *Purity and danger: An analysis of concepts of pollution and taboo*. New York, NY: Praeger.

25 Durkheim, E. (1965). *The elementary forms of the religious life*. New York, NY: Free Press.

26 Marx, K. (1965). *Capital: a critical analysis of capitalistic production* (Vol. 3). Moscow: Progress Publishers.

27 Lamont, M., & Molnár, V. (2002). The study of boundaries in the social sciences. *Annual review of sociology, 28*, 167–195.

28 Zerubavel, E. (2009). *Social mindscapes: An invitation to cognitive sociology*. Cambridge, MA: Harvard University Press.

29 Archer, M., Bhaskar, R., Collier, A., Lawson, T., & Norrie, A. (2013). *Critical realism: Essential readings*. New York: Routledge.

30 Gorski, P. S. (2013). What is critical realism? And why should you care? *Contemporary Sociology: A Journal of Reviews, 42*(5), 658–670.

31 Giddens, A. (1984). *The constitution of society: Outline of the theory of structuration*. Berkeley, CA: University of California Press.

32 Archer, M. S. (1995). *Realist social theory: The morphogenetic approach*. Cambridge: Cambridge University Press.

33 Hofstadter, Douglas R. (1999), Gödel, Escher, Bach. New York : Basic Books.

34 Wallerstein, I. (2004). *World-systems analysis: An introduction*. Durham, NC: Duke University Press.

35 Thatcher, M. (1987). No such thing as society. *An Interview with Douglas Keay*, (10), 8–10.

36 Lama, D. (2001). *Ethics for the new millennium*. New York, NY: Riverhead Books.

37 Macut, I. (2015). Fraternity, the foundation and pathway to peace. Message of his Holiness Francis for the celebration of the World Day of Peace. A brief explanation and actualization. *Diacovensia, 22*(4), 559–575.

38 Pinker, S. (2011). *The better angels of our nature: Why violence has declined*. New York, NY: Viking.

39 Stark, R., & Bainbridge, W. S. (1987). *A theory of religion* (Vol. 2). New York: Lang.

40 Winokur, J. (2005). *Zen to go: Bite-sized bits of wisdom* (p. 240). Seattle, WA: Sasquatch Books.

41 Stein, R. M., Post, S. S., & Rinden, A. L. (2000). Reconciling context and contact effects on racial attitudes. *Political Research Quarterly, 53*(2), 285–303.

42 Sigelman, L., & Welch, S. (1993). The contact hypothesis revisited: Black-white interaction and positive racial attitudes. *Social forces*, 781–795.

43 Merton, T. (1986). *The hidden ground of love: The letters of Thomas Merton on religious experience and social concerns*. New York: Farrar, Straus, Giroux.

44 Rabin, N. (2006). Stephen Colbert interview. The AV Club. Retrieved, 08-15. http://www.avclub.com/article/stephen-colbert-13970

45 Diamond, L., & Plattner, M. F. (2012). *Liberation technology: Social media and the struggle for democracy*. Baltimore, MD: JHU Press.

46 Huxley, A. (1958). *Brave new world revisited*. New York, NY: Harper & Brothers.

47 Przybylski, A. K., Murayama, K., DeHaan, C. R., & Gladwell, V. (2013). Motivational, emotional, and behavioral correlates of fear of missing out. *Computers in Human Behavior*, *29* (4), 1841–1848.

48 Stephens, M., Yoo, J., Mourao, R. R., Vu, H. T., Baresch, B., & Johnson, T. J. (2014). How App Are People to Use Smartphones, Search Engines, and Social Media for News?: Examining Information Acquisition Tools and Their Influence on Political Knowledge and Voting. *Journal of Information Technology & Politics*, *11*(4), 383–396.

49 Hesse, H. (1974). *Demian: Die Geschichte von Emil Sinclairs Jugend* (1. Aufl. ed.). Frankfurt am Main: Suhrkamp.

50 Einstein, A., & Dukas, H. (1981). *Albert Einstein, the human side: New glimpses from his archives*. Princeton, NJ: Princeton University Press.

51 Coleman, J. W. (2002). *The new Buddhism: The western transformation of an ancient tradition*. New York: Oxford University Press.

52 Another is the highly influential Harvard sociologist Pitirim Sorokin, who was such a beloved mentor that hundreds of students wore "Sorokin Lives!" buttons to the 1969 American Sociological Association meetings, one year after his death.

53 Foucault, M., & Sheridan, A. (1972). *The archaeology of knowledge*. New York, NY: Pantheon Books.

54 Winokur, J. (2005). *Zen to go: Bite-sized bits of wisdom*. Seattle, WA: Sasquatch Books.

55 Flexner, S. B. (1987). *Random House dictionary of the English language*. New York: Random House.

56 Aristotle. (350 BC)(2012). *Nicomachean ethics*. Oxford, UK: Acheron Press.

57 Hursthouse, R. (1999). *On virtue ethics*. Oxford, UK: Oxford University Press.

58 Aristotle. (350 BC)(2012). *Nicomachean ethics*. Oxford, UK: Acheron Press.

59 Hursthouse, R. (1999). *On virtue ethics*. Oxford, UK: Oxford University Press.

60 Iyer, P. (2009). *The open road: the global journey of the fourteenth Dalai Lama*. New York: Vintage Books.

61 Peterson, C., & Seligman, M. E. (2004). Character strengths and virtues: A handbook and classification. Oxford University Press.

62 Twenge, J. M., & Campbell, W. K. (2009). *The narcissism epidemic: Living in the age of entitlement*. Simon & Schuster, New York, NY.

63 McDonald, N. M., & Messinger, D. S. (2011). The development of empathy: How, when, and why. *Moral Behavior and Free Will: A Neurobiological and Philosophical Approach*, 341–368.

64 Ebert, R. (2012). *Awake in the dark: The best of Roger Ebert*. Chicago: University of Chicago Press.

65 Donaldson, D. M. (1963) "Conversations of Muhammad" *Studies in Muslim Ethics*. London: S.P.C.K, p. 82.

66 Barro, Robert and Jong-Wha Lee. (April 2010). A new data set of educational attainment in the world, 1950–2010. *Journal of Development Economics*, *104*, 184–198.

67 Perna, L. W. (2010). *Understanding the working college student: New research and its implications for policy and practice*. Sterling: Stylus Publishing, LLC.

68 Kena, G., Musu-Gillette, L., Robinson, J., Wang, X., Rathbun, A., Zhang, J., Wilkinson-Flicker, S., Barmer, A., & Dunlop Velez, E. (2015). *The condition of education* 2015 (NCES 2015-144). U.S. Department of Education, National Center for Education Statistics. Washington, DC.

69 Fromm, E., & Anshen, R. (1956). *The art of loving.* New York, NY: Harper & Row.

70 Rast, D., & Lebell, S. (1998). *Music of silence: A sacred journey through the hours of the days.* Berkeley, CA: Seastone.

71 Emmons, R. A., & Crumpler, C. A. (2000). Gratitude as a human strength: Appraising the evidence. *Journal of Social and Clinical Psychology, 19*(1), 56–69.